LABRADOR RETRIEVER INSIGHTS

TRAINING, HEALTH, CHAOS AND REALITY...

THE *UNFILTERED* LABRADOR RETRIEVER GUIDE

ZERO
WOOFS
GIVEN
PRESS

Labrador Retriever Insights

Written by Zero Woofs Given Press

Part of the Zero Woofs Dog Breed Library series

For permission requests, write to the publisher at:

Rowan's Publishing, LLC
Grass Valley, California
www.zerowoofsgiven.com

contact@zerowoofsgiven.com

Second Edition: 2025

Cover and interior design by Zero Woofs Given Press
Printed in the United States of America

Disclaimer

This book is intended for informational purposes only. It is not a substitute for professional veterinary, training, or legal advice. Always consult with qualified professionals regarding the care, training, and health of your dog.

DEDICATION

For every Labrador who ever wagged through the storm,
and for every human who didn't give up when it got hard.

For the ones who came home covered in mud, smelled like fish,
and still got a "good boy" anyway.

For the rescues who were written off,
and the owners who decided "not this time."

For the people who traded their clean houses, free time,
and personal boundaries for loyalty you can feel in your bones.

OTHER GUIDES AVAILABLE FROM THE ZERO WOOFS GIVEN DOG BREED LIBRARY

-Woof-a-Pedia: The Brutally Honest Dog Breed Guide
-Rottweiler Insights
-Great Dane Insights

BOOKS COMING SOON

-French Bulldog Insights
-German Shepherd Dog Insights
-Golden Retriever Insights
-English Bulldog Insights

TABLE OF CONTENTS

INTRODUCTION

Every damn week, another Labrador hits a shelter.
Different dog, same excuse.
"Too much energy."
"Needs more time than we thought."
"Great dog, just not the right fit."

Translation: *we screwed up*.

Nobody wants to admit they bought the fantasy. The commercials. The Instagram posts. The family down the street with their calm old Lab who plays fetch like a dream. What people don't see is the shredded couch it took to get there, or the ten thousand "no's" that dog heard before it earned that halo.

I've been in the dog world over twenty years—vet tech, trainer, rescue rehabber, chaos wrangler. I've had Labs pee on me, Labs flatten me, Labs look me dead in the eye while eating drywall like popcorn. You think you've seen destruction? Try watching a seventy-five-pound Labrador redecorate a kitchen in under five minutes because you thought a "quick trip to Target" didn't need a crate.

Here's the hard truth: the Labrador Retriever isn't broken; **people are**. We bred the perfect working machine and then got pissed when it didn't want to binge Netflix.

Labs were made to *do things*—haul nets, fetch game, dive into freezing water because their human pointed and said "go." They're smart, obsessive, and built for motion. They are absolutely not designed for your nine-to-five lifestyle and decorative throw pillows. When you take that kind of drive and give it nothing to do, you don't get a calm pet; you get a furry anarchist with separation anxiety and a taste for baseboards.

I've watched it over and over: the sweet puppy that turns into "too much dog," the once-excited family that ghosts their trainer, the surrender form filled out in shaky handwriting. The dog doesn't understand any of it. It just sits there, tail thumping, waiting for the life it was promised.

This book exists to stop that. Not to romanticize. Not to scold. To tell the truth.

You'll get the real Labrador here—the hunger, the humor, the chaos, and the cost. You'll see why the dog that greets you like a long-lost friend can also drive you to the edge of madness. You'll learn why training isn't optional, why structure means survival, and why this breed, when done right, will ruin you for every other kind of dog.

If you want a Labrador because they're "good with kids" or "easy to train," close this book and buy a stuffed animal instead. But if you're ready for a dog that will test you, match you, and love you harder than you thought possible, keep reading.

You're about to learn what the brochures left out. And if you still bring home a Lab after that, I respect the hell out of you.

Chapter 1
The Real History of
the Labrador Retriever

Every week another Lab lands in a shelter, tail still
wagging, owner still lying.
"Too energetic."
"Needs more time than we thought."
"Great dog, just not the right fit."

All translation for one thing: we didn't do our homework.

People talk about Labradors like they're plug-and-play.
They forget this breed wasn't born in a Pottery Barn catalog.
It started in the 1500s off the coast of Newfoundland, in
weather so cold it could kill a man in minutes. Back then
English and Portuguese fishermen ran the cod trade, and
every one of them needed a dog tough enough to survive
the North Atlantic. Those early dogs were mutts—
European water spaniels, Portuguese working dogs, maybe
a touch of collie—built by necessity, not pedigree. They
were called **St. John's Water Dogs**, after the capital of
Newfoundland: short-coated, black with white socks, small
enough to leap in and out of rowboats, smart enough to find
a dropped fish before it sank, and loyal enough to follow
their human into hell if that's where the nets went.

That dog was the ancestor of every Labrador alive today. It
didn't give a damn about "temperament tests." Its job was
to haul wet nets, drag ropes through surf, and save
fishermen from drowning. At night it slept in the boats,
covered in salt and fish slime, dreaming of the next catch.
That's the original Labrador—half otter, half engine.

By the early 1800s, ships from England were running
constant trade to Newfoundland. The British were obsessed
with dogs that could retrieve shot game without mangling

it. They saw the locals' water dogs working and lost their minds. The **Earl of Malmesbury**, the **Earl of Home**, and the **Duke of Buccleuch** began importing them through the port of **Poole, Dorset**. Around 1823 Malmesbury wrote that he'd been breeding his "Labrador dogs" from Newfoundland imports for years; that's the first written use of the name. It stuck because the dogs came through Labrador as part of the shipping route.

The British, of course, couldn't leave anything alone. They turned work into sport and sport into status. They crossed those hard-working water dogs with their own hunting stock—setters and pointers mainly—to create the perfect gentleman's retriever. The fisherman's partner became the aristocrat's accessory. The new version was still tough, still eager, but a little prettier, a little calmer, and much more acceptable around the dinner table.

The only thing that changed was the marketing. The drive stayed. The stamina stayed. The bottomless obsession to carry things stayed. The English just dressed it in manners and called it refinement.

By the mid-1800s, the Labrador had become the retriever of choice for Britain's shooting estates. Malmesbury's dogs were famous for taking hand signals across water and bringing back birds without crushing them. The Duke of Buccleuch kept his line in Scotland. These men weren't sentimental; they were practical. If a dog couldn't work, it didn't breed. That ruthless efficiency forged the mind we still see in every modern Lab—the focus, the eagerness, the terrifying mix of sensitivity and obsession.

When the **Kennel Club** recognized the Labrador Retriever in 1903, the split began. Hunters wanted performance; the show crowd wanted uniformity. Pretty dogs win ribbons, ribbons sell puppies, and purpose slides to the back seat. Early field trials in Britain still tested grit—ten-hour days in marshes followed by a calm heel at dinner—but city folks saw those same dogs and thought, *what a lovely companion for the children.*

By the time the breed crossed fully into America in the early 1900s, the rot was already setting in. We took the world's best working retriever and tried to make it a suburban babysitter. That's where every modern problem begins.

The St. John's dogs vanished by the 1980s—extinct because no one needed them anymore—but their ghosts live in every Labrador's DNA. You can still see them when a Lab hits the water like it's coming home or can't walk past a puddle without testing it. That's four hundred years of instinct, not misbehavior.

People ask why Labs are obsessed with carrying things. Easy. Centuries of fishermen rewarded the dogs that brought stuff back. Those genes don't disappear because you moved into a condo. The soft mouth, the compulsion to grab, the joy of having something—anything—in their teeth—it's history repeating itself in your living room. You can fight it or respect it.

Across the 1900s the divide widened. On one side stood the field people—hunters, handlers, die-hards who still judged a dog by how it worked. On the other side were the show folks—kennel-club hobbyists chasing symmetry and giant heads. Field dogs stayed lean, wired, intense. Show dogs got heavier, slower, prettier. Both sides swore theirs was the "true" Labrador, which is hilarious because neither one could survive a week on a Newfoundland fishing boat.

By the 1920s field-trial culture was booming across Britain, keeping some working sanity alive. Then Americans got involved.

The first official Labs landed here around the turn of the century, imported by wealthy hunters who wanted bragging rights. For a while they kept the balance: sleek black dogs that could swim all day and still heel like soldiers. But America can ruin anything with marketing.

After World War II the suburbs exploded. People wanted family dogs, not hunting partners. The Labrador fit the image perfectly—short hair, big smile, not scary. Black Labs were everywhere. Then yellow was "friendlier." Then chocolate was "rare." Breeders realized color sold better than character. That was the beginning of the modern mess.

By the 1970s, Labs had become the go-to "safe" breed. Every ad campaign, every movie, every cereal box used them as a mascot for wholesomeness. Disney turned them into saints. AKC registrations skyrocketed, quality nose-dived. Backyard breeders cranked them out like widgets because people would pay for them. Why bother screening hips or temperaments when cash came faster than common sense?

Here's the part no one likes to say out loud: the Lab's good-natured rep made it a target. That softness made them easy to exploit. Puppy mills jumped on board, the gene pool shrank, and we started getting fat Labs, nervous Labs, aggressive Labs, dumb Labs—all wearing a reputation they didn't earn.

Field lines evolved separately. The American field Lab became a missile—skinny, fast, relentless. Brilliant, yes, but too much dog for the average human. I've worked them; they'll go through a wall if you throw a bumper over it. The show lines went the other direction—barrel-bodied, slower, bred for "sweetness." People call them calmer. They're not. They're just lazier and arthritic by five.

Both camps built caricatures of the same animal. The balance that made the original Labrador perfect—a dog with drive *and* sense—got lost somewhere between the gun field and the grooming table.

Then came the color fads. If you ever need proof that humanity's doomed, look at the "silver Lab." Somebody figured out a Weimaraner cross could pass as "rare" and slapped a luxury label on it. Boom—instant profit. I've trained some of those dogs: nice enough, but half carry health baggage—skin issues, weak joints, anxiety. The silver craze turned an already-wobbling gene pool into a genetic yard sale.

And people kept buying them. Because humans love lies wrapped in fur.

You can't blame the dogs. They didn't ask to be mass-produced or "designer." They're just doing what they were wired to do—move, retrieve, connect. The tragedy is how far we've drifted from respecting that wiring.

Watch a good working Lab and you'll see ghosts. That coat sheds water like oil. The tail works like a rudder. The nose can track scent underwater. Every part of that body was built for a reason—centuries of selective breeding for utility, not aesthetics. A fisherman from 1700 wouldn't recognize today's pudgy couch Labs, but he'd recognize the look in their eyes: *tell me what to do and I'll do it.*

That's the piece most owners never grasp. The Labrador's heart was forged in labor, not leisure. You can't obedience-class that history away. It's still there, humming under the surface. When your dog drags you toward a lake or obsessively drops a tennis ball at your feet until your shoulder gives out, that's not disobedience. That's four hundred years of genetic memory screaming for a job.

And yet we keep setting them up to fail. We take this workhorse and lock it in an apartment. We feed it out of boredom and call the resulting obesity "love." We brag about its friendliness while ignoring its anxiety. We break their spirit with neglect, then dump them when they chew a doorframe. And somehow, we still call ourselves dog lovers.

I've lost count of how many Labs I've seen broken by good intentions. Families wanting "the perfect kid dog." Couples thinking a Lab would "get them outside more." Hunters buying Craigslist puppies because "it looked like a good line." Half those dogs ended up confused, overweight, or surrendered before their second birthday.

History explains every one of those failures. You can't take a creature bred to work the roughest coastlines on Earth and expect it to sit quietly while you scroll TikTok. You can't remove purpose and expect peace. The Labrador Retriever was engineered by necessity, perfected by discipline, and destroyed by convenience.

The early fishermen didn't care about companionship; they cared about survival. The British gentry didn't care about therapy dogs; they cared about shooting birds. Every generation of humans used this breed for something practical. We're the first to use it for nothing—and it shows.

If you want to honor the Labrador's history, don't hang its portrait. Give it a purpose. Train it, swim it, make it retrieve, make it think. Remind it what it was built to be. That's the only way this breed survives with its dignity intact.

So next time your Lab wakes you at dawn with a toy jammed in your face, don't yell. That's history talking. The same instincts that pulled nets in Newfoundland and fetched pheasants for lords are what drive your dog to shove a slobbery ball at your ribs. You asked for a Labrador. This is the deal.

The breed isn't broken. We are. But history gave us the blueprint to fix it—if we'd stop pretending they're plush toys and start treating them like the working partners they were born to be.

Dress it up, give it fancy colors, slap it on cereal boxes, call it "America's favorite dog." Underneath all that branding is a creature that still belongs to the sea, the field, and the hunt. The day we forget that is the day we lose the Labrador completely.

So, when your dog barrels into the lake, tail spinning, eyes bright, water flying in all directions—don't pull it back. Let it go. That's four centuries of breeding doing exactly what it was meant to do. That's the real Labrador.

Chapter 2
The Labrador Operating System

That's the truth no one puts on the brochure. And speaking of truth, let's talk about what's actually going on between those floppy ears.

You think you know what's in there—loyalty, sweetness, maybe a few extra neurons dedicated to tennis balls—but that brain is a carnival ride built by drunk engineers. The Labrador mind is equal parts genius, clown, and con artist. It runs on emotion, food, and opportunity, which means it's brilliant one second and a full-on toddler riot the next.

Labs don't think like other breeds. They feel first, act second, and think… eventually. They're emotional sponges with the impulse control of a sugar-high preschooler. You sigh; they sigh. You're anxious; they start pacing. You eat junk; they'll try to eat the wrapper. They mirror you so closely it's unsettling, like someone downloaded your worst habits into a 70-pound creature with better hair.

That sensitivity is what makes them amazing workers. A Labrador was bred to read human micro-signals—the twitch of a hand, a whistle, a tone shift. They feel the mood before you do. That's also why they're masters of emotional blackmail. They weaponize empathy. They can tell when you're guilty, and they'll milk it until you apologize for going to work.

Labs are manipulative geniuses wrapped in fur. Inside that smile is a creature running three cons at once: "I'm starving," "I'm lonely," and "I'm innocent." They're all lies, and you'll believe every one. The guilt eyes? Evolutionary warfare. Those soulful stares were fine-tuned over centuries to make fishermen share dinner and hunters toss scraps. You don't stand a chance.

But the real chaos starts when a Lab gets bored. Boredom is their supervillain origin story. A bored Labrador can take down a house faster than termites with caffeine. I've seen drywall eaten, couches flayed, and car seats excavated to the frame. They don't do it out of spite—they do it because their brain is wired for constant problem-solving, and you gave them no problems to solve. They'll make their own.

Here's the cruel joke: the smarter the Lab, the worse the destruction. Dumb ones chew socks; smart ones learn how to open fridges, pull child locks, and rearrange your pantry. I once met a dog who figured out how to turn on the kitchen faucet. Twice. The owners came home to a flooded house and a Labrador floating in the glory of his own intelligence.

People love to call Labs "easy." They're not easy—they're *compliant.* There's a difference. A Lab will cooperate, sure, but only if it sees the point. Tell it to fetch? Done. Tell it to stop eating the drywall? You'd better have a better offer. Training a Lab isn't about dominance; it's about negotiation. You're not a master; you're a project manager.

Their minds are wired like Velcro: once something sticks, good luck pulling it off. That's why they're such reliable workers and such persistent idiots. Teach one to retrieve and it'll do it forever. Let one steal a sock and it'll collect laundry like a dragon hoarding gold. Every Lab on earth has an internal list of "approved thefts"—socks, dish towels, children's toys, whatever gets a reaction. They live for reactions.

The mouth obsession? That's centuries of conditioning. Those Newfoundland ancestors carried ropes and nets through surf; their descendants carried birds through marshes. You can't breed that out just because you like clean carpets. The Lab's mouth is its tool, its comfort, its hobby, its emotional support system. When it carries your shoe around, it's not being bad—it's self-soothing. Unfortunately, that comfort item used to cost you $120.

And then there's food. Labs don't *like* food; they *worship* it. The survival instincts of fishing dogs who lived on scraps turned into a religion of gluttony. They don't stop eating because their body never evolved an off switch. You can see the desperation in their eyes: *Eat now or die later.* That's why so many of them are shaped like footstools by age six. Humans confuse appetite with affection. The Lab doesn't need another treat—it needs structure. But structure requires guilt-free humans, and those are extinct.

The average owner thinks love will compensate for discipline. It doesn't. A Lab without clear rules turns feral fast. Not aggressive—just wild, chaotic, running entirely on emotion and momentum. They'll jump fences, counter-surf, and break into closets for fun. You can't punish them for it either. They don't connect your outrage with their action; they just think you've lost your mind again.

Labs also hold grudges for about eight seconds. You yell, they flinch, then they're back with a toy. They live in emotional real-time. That's why they're great therapy dogs and terrible poker players. They can't fake anything. Whatever they feel comes blasting out of their bodies like confetti.

But here's the dangerous part—because they read us so well, they become emotional mirrors. You get a lazy Lab when you're lazy. You get an anxious Lab when you're a control freak. You get a confident, balanced Lab when you actually do the work. They reflect who you are, not who you want to be. That's why they break so many people's hearts. The dog ends up being the truth you didn't want to see.

Every trainer I know says the same thing: you don't *train* a Lab; you *raise* one. You guide it through choices like a toddler. You redirect, reward, and repeat until its chaos turns into competence. You have to manage emotion before behavior. Because this breed isn't logical—it's relational. They don't obey commands; they follow feelings.

They're also dramatic as hell. A stubbed paw? Tragic. A missed meal? Abuse. Leave them home alone for more than three hours, and you'll come back to a Shakespearean tragedy performed in shredded upholstery. The term "Velcro dog" exists because of them. They don't want to be near you; they want to *merge* with you. It's flattering until you realize you can't even pee without a Labrador escort.

The clinginess isn't weakness—it's wiring. For centuries they were bred to work shoulder-to-shoulder with humans, responding to every cue. Being alone feels unnatural. That's why so many develop separation anxiety. They're not needy; they're displaced. You took a pack-bonded working animal and dropped it into solitary confinement. The destruction that follows isn't defiance; it's panic with teeth.

If you've ever come home to a demolished room and a Lab sitting in the wreckage with "that face," here's the truth: it's not guilt—it's reading your fury. They don't feel moral shame; they feel tension. They're watching your micro-expressions and bracing for impact. The "guilty Lab" meme? It's just a dog preemptively begging you not to lose it.

Living with one is a daily negotiation between love and damage control. You'll adore them while plotting their demise. They'll make you laugh while ruining your carpet. You'll swear off dogs forever—then melt when they rest their head on your knee. They're emotional black holes; they suck all rational thought out of a room.

Every Lab owner learns the same lesson sooner or later: affection and destruction are the same impulse in different outfits. They chew the things they love. They smother the people they love. They don't know moderation. You tell them to relax, and they hear, *intensify affection immediately.*

A Labrador in balance is a masterpiece—loyal, tireless, empathetic, stupidly joyful. A Labrador without direction is a one-dog hurricane. The difference is leadership, not luck. Give them structure, and they'll move mountains. Give them freedom without purpose, and they'll redecorate your life in confetti.

You can see it in their eyes: that mix of joy, guilt, and calculation. They're planning their next move even as they lean into your hand. There's something human about it, which is why we forgive them every time. They remind us of ourselves at our worst—hungry, impulsive, craving connection, desperate to be good but not entirely sure how.

So when your Lab drops a slimy tennis ball in your lap for the 400th time, take the hint. It's not just fetch; it's therapy. When it nudges your hand during a fight, it's not meddling; it's diffusing tension. When it eats your sandwich right off the counter, it's… well, that one's just theft, but at least it's consistent.

The Labrador mind isn't broken. It's just running software designed for a world that doesn't exist anymore—a world of work, partnership, and constant feedback. We replaced that with long workdays and Netflix. No wonder they're losing their minds.

So if you live with one, remember this: you didn't buy a decoration. You hired an employee and forgot to give it a job. Give that brain something to do—training, swimming, nose work, puzzle toys, anything. A tired Lab is a good Lab; a bored Lab is a demolition expert.

They'll never stop testing boundaries, and honestly, you wouldn't want them to. That spark of mischief is what makes them alive. It's what made them human partners for five centuries. Every bit of chaos they bring into your home is just a reminder of how deep that bond runs.

They'll frustrate you, make you laugh, and occasionally make you cry—but if you stick it out, you'll end up with something rare: a creature that understands you better than you understand yourself. That's the deal you made the day you brought home a Labrador. It's not obedience you're buying; it's a mirror that wags its tail.

So yeah, they're sweet, smart, and slightly unhinged. But you'd miss the madness if it ever stopped. And deep down, you know it.

Chapter 3
Nature Made a Machine, Humans Made a Mess

You can't talk about a Lab's brain without talking about where it came from, and who's been screwing with it. The truth is, half of what you're dealing with came baked in at birth. The other half? You nurtured it, rewarded it, and called it cute. Congratulations. You've built a chaos engine with fur.

Every Labrador walking this earth is the product of a few centuries of selective insanity. The genes are the hardware. The environment is the operating system. And most people are running the wrong damn software.

Let's start with nature. A Labrador's DNA is still screaming orders from the North Atlantic: *Work. Fetch. Move. Please your human. Do something.* That drive doesn't turn off just because someone decided you'd look good in matching family pajamas. It's ancient programming. You can dull it, misdirect it, or ignore it, but you can't delete it.

When you look at a Labrador, you're looking at a dog whose ancestors hauled nets in freezing water, sprinted through marshes, and took hand signals across fog and gunfire. That kind of intensity doesn't just vanish. It leaks out of every cell. The modern "family Lab" still has a worker's heart and a marathoner's motor, but we've boxed it into backyards and apartments and wonder why it's losing its mind.

The field-bred Labs, the ones still closest to that original blueprint, are rockets with fur. Sleek, muscular, running on caffeine and compulsion. They're not "hyper." They're built for constant purpose. A true field Lab can handle ten-hour hunting days, leap into icy water, track a bird you only imagined you hit, and beg for another round. When those dogs end up in suburban homes with nothing to do, they go nuclear.

The show-bred Labs? Different disaster, same reason. They're slower, thicker, bred for looks and "temperament." But that drive never really left. It just got buried under body fat and boredom. They still need work, but people mistake sluggishness for calmness. Then they overfeed them, undertrain them, and end up with a 90-pound toddler that farts in its sleep and chews baseboards out of frustration.

That's the paradox: we've bred a working dog without a job, then act shocked when it starts freelancing. Every hole in your yard, every shredded cushion, every "mystery object" retrieved from the trash is a symptom of that design mismatch. You didn't get a pet; you got a performance animal forced into retirement before its first paycheck.

And it's not just the breed's drive—it's the wiring. Genetics loads the gun, environment pulls the trigger. The wrong combo turns good instincts into bad behavior. You can trace half the Labrador "problems" I see back to one of three human screwups: bad breeding, bad environment, or bad expectations. Usually all three.

Let's start with the breeders, because someone has to. For every responsible one testing hips, elbows, and temperaments, there are a hundred backyard idiots whose idea of "good bloodlines" is two dogs that both have eyes. They'll breed anything that humps and call it "family raised." They don't know drive, balance, or nerve. They just know profit. That's how we got generations of anxious, overweight, poorly structured dogs that can't swim straight or focus for more than 10 seconds.

And don't get me started on color breeders. "Silver," "charcoal," "champagne", whatever shiny word they're using this week, it's all just marketing for watered-down genetics. You can practically hear the DNA groaning. Breeding for color instead of character is how you end up with Labs that look good on Instagram and fall apart everywhere else.

Even good breeders screw up when they breed for looks over brains. Show champions aren't necessarily stable. You can have perfect angulation and zero common sense. Beauty doesn't retrieve ducks. I've seen Labs with pedigrees a mile long who couldn't find a tennis ball in a bathtub.

But even a great breeder can't save a dog from a lousy home. Environment can warp even the best genetics. Too many people treat Labradors like living furniture. They think because the breed's "good-natured," it'll raise itself. It won't. It'll raise hell.

The most common story I hear? "He was so calm as a puppy!" Yeah, because he was exhausted from growing bones. Give it six months and that adorable lump turns into a hormone-charged freight train. Suddenly, the same people who praised its energy are calling trainers because "he's out of control." No, Karen. He's just a Labrador.

These dogs are emotional athletes. They thrive on consistency, exercise, and leadership. Remove those and you get chaos. You can't stick them in a crate for ten hours, walk them once around the block, and expect zen. They'll eat your drywall just to feel something.

It's not about dominance or punishment, it's about management. A Labrador's brain is built like a Formula One car. High performance, low patience. It needs steering. If you don't give it a job, it'll invent one, and you won't like the results. Most of what people call "bad behavior" is just misplaced drive. The dog's not being an asshole; it's trying to fulfill instincts you've given no outlet.

You see this all the time in field-bred dogs sold as pets. They need miles of movement, mental stimulation, and clear structure. Without it, they unravel. The worst cases are the ones rehomed three times before they're two years old— each owner less equipped than the last. Everyone blames the dog, but the problem started the day someone thought a working-line Lab would make a nice couch accessory.

The show-bred ones aren't immune either. They're more mellow but still need leadership. Their energy leaks out in sneaky ways: counter-surfing, door-bolting, compulsive licking. They'll act lazy until something triggers them— doorbell, squirrel, pizza delivery—and suddenly you've got a bulldozer in motion. They may move slower, but they crash harder.

And let's not forget the "it's just a phase" crowd. These are the people who excuse every disaster until the dog's too far gone to fix. The Lab that jumps? "He's just excited." The Lab that guards toys? "He's just protective." The Lab that drags them down the street? "He's strong!" No. He's untrained. You're lazy. And now he's a danger to himself and everyone else.

Behavior is never random—it's communication. A Lab that chews, jumps, or digs isn't misbehaving; it's sending you a message in destruction form. The problem is humans keep deleting the message instead of reading it.

And here's the kicker: even when people get a warning, they don't learn. They'll lose one Lab to chaos, swear off the breed, then buy another puppy "from a calmer line." Spoiler: it's not calmer. You just repeated the same mistakes.

Nature versus nurture isn't a contest—it's a collaboration. You can't control the genes, but you can sure as hell control what you do with them. Training isn't optional for this breed; it's oxygen. Socialization isn't a suggestion; it's insurance. You don't "fix" a Labrador; you channel it.

I've worked field lines that could drive you insane with their intensity and show lines that could out-stubborn a mule. Both types can be brilliant, loyal, and steady—but only if their humans understand what they bought. That's the part no breeder brochure covers: you're not just choosing color or size; you're choosing engine type. Get a field-bred Lab and you're signing up for a turbocharged project. Get a show-bred one and you're signing up for a diesel truck with a brain. Both need maintenance, both can destroy you financially, and both will break your heart if you treat them like toys.

And then there's the backyard wildcard—dogs bred for nothing but demand. Those are the real heartbreakers. Unstable temperaments, joint issues, allergies, anxiety. They come from places where no one knows or cares what makes a Labrador *a Labrador*. They just want a fast sale. Those dogs deserve better than the world they're born into, but the only way to fix it is to stop buying them.

That's the hard truth people don't want to hear: every bad breeder stays in business because people keep paying them. If you buy a cheap puppy "to save it," you didn't rescue it—you funded the next litter. Every dollar spent on irresponsibility guarantees more broken dogs.

The fix starts before the leash is even bought. Research lines. Meet breeders. Look for health tests, not color charts. Don't fall for buzzwords like "English" and "American" like they mean quality—they're marketing shorthand. Ask what the parents *do*. If the breeder can't answer, walk away.

When you finally bring that puppy home, remember: it's not a blank slate. It's a four-century-old program wrapped in baby fat. You're not "training" it so much as directing ancient instincts into something that won't destroy your drywall. It's nature and nurture shaking hands and agreeing to chaos management.

Owning a Labrador is like owning a sports car—you can't blame the engine for going fast. You can only blame yourself for not learning to drive.

So when your Lab's bouncing off the walls, shredding toys, and testing every boundary you've got, don't ask "what's wrong with him." Ask "what did I do to create this." Responsibility doesn't start when the leash snaps on; it starts the moment you decide to bring that heartbeat home.

Because at the end of the day, a Labrador doesn't care about your excuses. It only cares about what you teach, what you reward, and how much of its chaos you can handle with love and patience. Nature gave you the blueprint. Nurture decides whether it becomes a masterpiece or a demolition site.

The dog's not the problem. It's the mirror. And when you finally stop blaming genetics and start looking at the reflection staring back, you'll realize the hardest part of owning a Labrador isn't training the dog—it's training yourself. Which brings us to the uncomfortable question every would-be Lab owner needs to answer: are you actually built for this?

Chapter 4
The Lab Fantasy vs. The Lab Reality

You think you're ready. You've read the warnings, nodded through the truth bombs, maybe even convinced yourself you're different, that you'll be the one who "does it right." Sure. That's what they all say.

Then the puppy arrives.

All that confidence evaporates the second seventy pounds of unfiltered Labrador destiny barrels into your life. You weren't prepared; no one ever is. And that's where this part starts—not with the fantasy of owning a Lab, but with the brutal, hilarious, hair-covered reality of surviving one.

You've seen the commercials. The sunshine, the picket fence, the kids giggling while a perfectly behaved Labrador trots across the yard. Lies. Every frame of that fantasy is brought to you by handlers, editing, and sedatives. The real version involves pee on the floor, teeth marks on the drywall, and someone crying in the laundry room. A Labrador's first two years are a contact sport.

I've watched it happen a hundred times. Family shows up all smiles, two parents, three kids, a Pinterest board full of "cute puppy names." They last four days before panic sets in. By week two the shoes are shredded, the toddler's screaming because the dog "nibbled," and Dad's standing in the yard at 5 a.m. whispering, "What have we done?" The commercial never shows that part.

Puppyhood isn't a montage. It's a siege. Labs are born as nuclear optimists with no concept of physics, pain, or property. They bite because they're happy, they jump because they love you, and they destroy because stillness feels like death. You don't raise a Lab; you survive it until the frontal lobe finally moves in around year three.

Every owner swears they'll "be consistent." Then come the sleepless nights, the razor-toothed land-shark stage, and the 11 p.m. zoomies that sound like a stampede. By month six they're crying into Google searches about monasteries and wondering if monks allow dogs.

Here's the truth: a Labrador puppy is a full-time job wearing fur. They don't care that you have work, plans, or a pulse. Their energy doesn't care that your day was long. It's a biological force, not a personality quirk. They were built to move, and if you can't keep up, you'll pay for it in drywall and therapy bills.

Exercise alone eliminates half the population. "Oh, but we have a backyard." Cute. That patch of grass isn't exercise; it's a toilet. A Lab needs miles, not minutes. Swimming, running, obedience, scent work—daily, not when your Fitbit guilts you. Skip it and they'll invent their own CrossFit program involving your couch cushions.

A normal morning in a Lab house goes like this: 6 a.m., the dog's awake and vibrating. You stumble outside in slippers while it runs victory laps around the yard with half a branch in its mouth. You throw a ball once; it looks at you like "that's it?" By 8 a.m. you're sweating, it's grinning, and your neighbors think you've joined a cult that worships cardio.

Then there's the hair. You can't own a Lab and be a neat freak. Their coat sheds like it's personal. Black, yellow, chocolate—it all ends up woven into your existence. I've found Lab hair in my car vents, in sealed bags of rice, once in a freezer. You don't vacuum it; you accept it as a new decorating style called "textured despair."

And the drool—good grief. Labs drool when they're happy, anxious, breathing, or existing. You'll get nose prints on glass, drool strings on jeans, and mysterious smears on walls at shoulder height. If you need pristine furniture, get a statue.

Personal space? Gone. You'll never pee alone again. They'll nudge doors open, sit in your lap, and rest their head on your keyboard mid-email. They don't want to be near you; they want to merge with you. If you're someone who values boundaries, this isn't your breed. They will crawl onto you like emotional weighted blankets, and you'll let them because those eyes short-circuit logic.

Now let's talk money. A Lab eats like a linebacker and racks up vet bills like a toddler with a death wish. Hips, ears, skin, stomach—they all need attention. Add training classes, chewed-through toys, and premium food, and you'll realize you basically adopted a furry car payment.

And yet, the biggest expense is time. They demand it. Without daily structure—real structure, not "we'll toss the ball for five minutes"—their brains turn feral. Consistency isn't optional; it's the leash holding your sanity together.

But here's the part people don't see coming: they reflect you. The dog that mirrors your best and worst habits. If you're anxious, they're wired. If you're lazy, they're destructive. If you're patient, they're brilliant. Labs don't adapt to your life; they expose it. That's what breaks people. The dog holds up the mirror, and you hate what you see.

I've seen every kind of incompatible owner.

The Neat Freak bleaches floors twice a day while the Lab gleefully redecorates with muddy paw prints. Therapy follows.

The Minimalist buys a white couch, a black dog, and learns despair is a color.

The Control Freak makes a daily schedule, only to watch the Lab eat it. Twice.

The Couch Potato tells me, "We'll just do short walks." Six months later they're being towed down the street like a water-skier.

Every one of them says the same thing: "He's so sweet, but he's driving us insane." No kidding. You adopted enthusiasm incarnate. This isn't a lifestyle accessory; it's a living engine with feelings.

And those feelings run deep. Labs are affection tyrants. They love you aggressively. They'll body-slam you out of joy. They'll crawl onto your chest mid-nap and stare until you acknowledge them. They weaponize love the way toddlers weaponize cuteness. You'll forgive them every time, which is why they own you.

But the madness has purpose. That relentless energy, that drive for contact—it's all history. Those instincts to follow, fetch, and stay close kept fishermen alive. Now they keep you moving when you'd rather rot on the couch. A Lab doesn't let you quit life. It drags you back into it.

Still, some people just shouldn't own one. If you hate exercise, noise, mud, or laughter at your expense, stay away. If you can't handle a creature that sheds, drools, steals underwear, and demands emotional availability, stay away. If you want your house to stay spotless or your mornings quiet, buy a Roomba.

A Lab's first two years will test every relationship in your house. I've seen marriages buckle under puppyhood. I've seen people cry because their "perfect family dog" turned out to be a furry cyclone. And then, slowly, if they stick it out, if they train, guide, and laugh instead of quit, it changes. Somewhere around year three, that chaos focuses. The manic energy melts into purpose. The fetch obsession becomes communication. The dog that once shredded furniture starts reading your thoughts. That's the reward for not giving up.

This is why I tell people: owning a Lab isn't about affection, it's about endurance. It's not a pet; it's a partnership. They don't care if you're tired, sad, or hungover—they still expect you to show up. They were bred to work beside humans no matter the weather or the mood. If you can't match that loyalty, don't sign the contract.

Let's get brutally honest. You want a Labrador because you want what it represents: loyalty, family, uncomplicated love. But those things aren't free. You earn them through exhaustion, consistency, and patience you didn't know you had. The calm, soulful dog in the commercials is built, not bought. Every peaceful old Lab you've ever met was once a chaotic maniac someone refused to give up on.

I've seen the other side too: the shelters full of dogs whose owners couldn't keep up. "Too much energy." "No time." "He needs a yard." No, he needed a leader. Every one of those surrenders started with good intentions and bad preparation. The Lab didn't fail. The humans did.

So here's your real compatibility quiz, no checkboxes, just honesty. Do you laugh when things break, or do you rage? Do you commit when it's hard, or look for shortcuts? Can you show up every single day, even when you don't feel like it? If you answered no to any of those, that's fine. Admitting it is kinder than pretending. Get a fish.

But if you read this and still feel something burning behind your ribs, if you're nodding through the warnings and thinking *yeah, bring it on,* then you might be one of the few built for this breed. Because when you match a Lab's chaos with your consistency, it turns into something extraordinary.

A balanced Labrador isn't calm because it's tired; it's calm because it trusts you. It knows the world makes sense when you're in it. That's the moment every owner fights for—the second you realize all the destruction was just communication on the way to understanding.

Owning a Lab won't make you a better person. It'll just make you more real. You'll stop pretending patience is easy, you'll learn to laugh at failure, and you'll find joy in the middle of mayhem. You'll track mud together, you'll curse together, and if you're lucky, you'll grow up together.

So before you sign that adoption form, look hard at your life. If you're ready to rebuild it around walks, laughter, and occasional property damage, then welcome. You're joining a centuries-old partnership that's messy, loud, and beautiful.

But if you're still clinging to the dream of a tidy house and quiet mornings, do everyone a favor. Don't ruin a good dog because you couldn't handle reality.

Because that's what this whole thing comes down to: it's not about getting the perfect dog, it's about being the right human. The Labrador already knows its part. The question is whether you're ready to meet it halfway.

If you are, tighten your laces and clear your schedule. The hard part's about to start.

CHAPTER 5
THE TRUE COST OF A LABRADOR (SPOILER: IT'S YOU)

Everyone wants the truth about Labradors until money enters the conversation. Then the room goes silent. People will nod while I talk about training, exercise, or commitment, but mention dollar signs and they suddenly look at the floor like kids getting "the talk."

So let's get real. Labradors are expensive. Not "a little pricey." Not "budget-friendly with planning." I mean expensive in the way weddings are expensive, where every decision adds another zero. That cute puppy is a ten-year payment plan with fur. You think the cost ends when you hand over the deposit? That was just the cover charge. The real bill shows up later, delivered in shredded furniture, vet receipts, and bags of food that cost more than your own groceries.

Watch a new Lab owner at the pet store. They walk in smiling; they walk out pale. The cart starts innocent enough—bowl, leash, food. Then comes the avalanche: crate, bed, toys, treats, shampoo, brushes, cleaning supplies for the urine apocalypse that's about to hit their house. By the time they hit the register, the puppy has chewed through the cart strap and they're $900 lighter. And they'll be back next week, because Labs eat toys for sport. You'll buy the "indestructible" ones and watch your dog prove marketing departments wrong in seven minutes flat. Eventually you just stand there muttering, "He's going to destroy it anyway," and grab whatever's on sale.

Food comes next. A Labrador can hear a kibble hit tile from two rooms away. Cheap food feels like a deal until the vet points out the skin issues, dull coat, and digestive disasters. Good kibble or fresh diets cost seventy to a hundred dollars a month, sometimes more. Multiply that by twelve months and ten years, and you've just fed a small car. And they don't stop at dog food. Labs treat the world as an all-you-can-eat buffet: socks, rocks, cat litter, remote controls, drywall, entire sandwiches, maybe a shoe for dessert. You'll learn new phrases like "foreign body surgery." That's a four-thousand-dollar way of saying "your dog ate something stupid again."

I once watched a Lab swallow a half loaf of bread, plastic bag and all, then look proud about it. The owner cried all the way to the emergency vet while the dog wagged his tail like he'd just won a medal. You'll try slow-feed bowls and puzzle feeders, but they'll master them faster than you can Google "how to stop a Labrador from inhaling dinner." Somewhere along the way you'll realize you're buying dog food in bulk like a restaurant.

Then the vet bills arrive. Vaccinations, heartworm pills, flea control, spay or neuter, annual bloodwork—that's just maintenance. The real money drains are hips, ears, and stomachs. Hips first. Labs are built like athletes and break down like them too. Hip dysplasia, arthritis, cruciate tears—pick your poison. Supplements, X-rays, pain meds, hydrotherapy, maybe surgery. Your "cheap puppy" turns into a $5,000 orthopedic project before middle age.

The ears are next. If you've never smelled a Labrador ear infection, count your blessings. Those floppy ears trap moisture like Tupperware. You'll clean them weekly, buy medicated drops, and still end up at the vet because "it smelled weird this morning." Every visit runs a few hundred dollars and they come in batches. Then there's the stomach, which is basically a garbage disposal with legs. They eat until they bloat, puke, or both. Bloat can kill. Surgery to fix it can cost three to eight thousand. If that doesn't make you rethink free feeding, nothing will.

Picture the vet waiting room. One Lab wearing a cone because he ate a sock. Another with a bandaged paw from chasing a ball through a fence. Someone trying to joke while mentally calculating what organ they can sell. You'll recognize them because one day you'll be them, holding your wallet like a hostage note.

Now multiply that scene by years. I once met a woman who adopted a two-year-old rescue Lab "to save money on puppy stuff." Within six months, she'd spent more on emergency vet care than a purebred pup from a responsible breeder would have cost. The dog had parasites, allergies, and anxiety. She didn't regret it, but she looked haunted every time she checked her bank balance.

Another couple called me after buying a "discount Lab" from a backyard breeder for four hundred bucks. By the time the dog turned one, he needed double knee surgery. Ten grand later, they stopped bragging about the deal.

Then there was Mike, single guy, city apartment, thought a Lab would be a "good way to get outside more." He was right—for a while. Then he started paying for daycare, walkers, vet insurance, and bigger rent. Last I heard, he had moved out of downtown and was pricing fences like a man who'd learned something the hard way.

Grooming looks simple until you live with one. That short coat lies. It sheds enough to knit another dog every spring. You'll vacuum daily and still leave the house covered in fur like you're starting a new fashion trend. Lint rollers become household décor. Baths, nail trims, ear cleanings, toothbrushes—none of it's optional. You'll pay someone to do it or sacrifice your Saturday afternoons to the cause.

Training? Same story. Group classes are a few hundred bucks, private lessons more. Skip them and you'll pay in repairs. Every Lab learns fast, but not on autopilot. Consistency costs energy and time, both of which you'll run out of before the dog does. People who "save money" by skipping training end up spending double on behaviorists later.

And then there's lifestyle. Want a weekend trip? Add boarding or a sitter. Want to move apartments? Add pet deposits and floor repairs. Vacations mean extra costs, and every piece of furniture becomes disposable. You think the dog is expensive; wait until you realize your whole life has to budget around it.

Hunters and sport owners? Whole new level. Training gear, bumpers, decoys, whistles, vests, waders. You'll own more waterproof equipment than a fisherman and a truck that looks like a kennel on wheels.

Then come the "oops" expenses. The phone screen cracked when the leash jerked. The couch ruined after one "small accident." The fence repaired because your dog decided freedom looked fun. None of that's in your spreadsheet, but it's all part of the deal.

And don't forget emotional spending. The guilt purchases. The organic treats, the orthopedic bed, the Christmas photoshoot. You'll tell yourself "he deserves it," while your card smokes from overuse. A Lab's eyes can make you bankrupt with pride. They run a scam older than currency itself: unconditional love for unlimited spending.

Add it up. Over a lifetime, a Labrador costs twenty to forty thousand dollars if you're lucky. More if you chase perfection with premium food and gold-standard vet care. You could buy a car, a degree, or half a house. Instead you'll have ten years of drool, fur, laughter, and chaos.

But the number doesn't even scratch the surface. It doesn't count midnight emergencies, lost deposits, or the rugs you sacrificed to puppyhood. It doesn't count the weekends you skip trips because you can't find a sitter or the vacation fund that became surgery money. It doesn't measure how your priorities change until "dog needs" and "family needs" mean the same thing.

Labs aren't money pits out of malice. They're money pits because they live at full speed. Their bodies are machines that burn calories, energy, and occasionally cash at terrifying rates. They don't do moderation. Every dent in your wallet mirrors the dents they put in your furniture and your patience.

And it doesn't stop at puppyhood. Age has its own invoice. Around year seven, the vet visits multiply. The hips start to creak, the walks slow down, the pills pile up. You'll buy joint supplements, pain meds, ramps for the car, rugs to keep them from slipping. Then come the senior blood panels, the x-rays, the "let's check that lump." By the end, you're not worried about the money; you're worried about time. You'll spend thousands to buy them another six months—and you'll do it without blinking. But the bills still come, and you still pay, because what else can you do?

Some owners buy pet insurance early and swear by it. Others buy it late and curse the exclusions. The rest gamble with savings and lose big. Even with coverage, you'll argue with claims departments like you're negotiating a hostage release. And just when you think you've seen it all, the modern "dog parent" economy shows up to finish the job. Birthday cakes, matching pajamas, GPS collars, doggy daycare, spa days. People laugh until they realize they're doing the same thing. Labs don't just drain wallets; they infect lifestyles.

I've watched people change jobs for their dogs. I've seen folks give up travel, move homes, even break relationships that couldn't handle "the dog comes first." It's not obsession; it's commitment. You start rearranging your life around the creature that rearranged your priorities. Work, friends, finances—all of it bends around that wagging center of gravity in your house.

Here's the hard truth. The price tag isn't the problem. The problem is pretending love alone pays the bills. You can adore your dog and still acknowledge the financial toll. Being realistic isn't cold; it's responsible. The honest owners aren't the ones who brag about saving money, they're the ones with an emergency fund labeled "stomach surgery."

You don't need to be rich to own a Lab. You need to be real. Budget for them like you'd budget for a kid who never moves out. They'll need food, healthcare, and attention every single day. You'll have to say no to some things because the dog comes first. Commitment isn't cute; it's expensive.

But when you do it right, the return is worth every penny. Labs don't care about your paycheck, your house, or your title. They care that you show up. They'll love you whether you're broke or comfortable as long as you're consistent. That kind of loyalty doesn't come cheap, and it shouldn't.

The people who cut corners always pay double. Skimp on food and you'll meet the dermatologist. Skip training and you'll meet the behaviorist. Ignore preventive care and you'll meet the surgeon. The breed doesn't forgive shortcuts.

Every great Lab I've met had an owner who paid the price willingly. Not just in money, but in time, effort, and humility. Every broken one came from someone who thought love was enough.

So before you fall for those brown eyes, do the math. Can you afford the food, the vet, the chaos, the endless stream of replacement toys? Can you handle the cost when age or bad luck shows up? Can you laugh when you're broke because the dog just ate another remote?

If you can, you'll be fine. You'll curse, you'll sweat, you'll swipe your card and mutter "worth it." And you'll mean it. Because every dollar you spend comes back in tail wags, muddy footprints, and that rare kind of joy you can't buy any other way.

If you can't, that's okay. Honesty is kinder than bankruptcy. Labradors deserve owners who can afford both the love and the lifestyle. Love doesn't pay the bills, but it's what makes paying them worth it.

Because that's the real cost. Not the money itself, but what it measures—the loyalty you buy with patience, the trust you build with sacrifice, the heartbreak you'll face when the bills stop because the dog is gone. That's the final payment, and it's the one that hurts the most.

CHAPTER 6
PREPARING FOR THE TORNADO

No one is ready for a Labrador puppy. People think they are. They've read the blogs, they've watched the "how to train your puppy" videos with chipper hosts holding angelic eight-week-olds that never bite, never bark, never drag a slipper across the carpet like a trophy. Those dogs exist only in marketing departments and heaven. The one you're about to bring home is a caffeinated tornado wearing fur.

The days before pickup feel like prepping for a baby, except the baby has teeth and an eating disorder. You walk through your house with optimism, looking for hazards. Ten minutes later you realize your entire home is a hazard. Cords, shoes, furniture legs, carpet fringe, baseboards, stair rails, even the wall corners. You start picking things up, taping things down, moving things higher, and still, deep inside, you know it's not enough. The Lab will find the one thing you forgot and destroy it while making direct eye contact.

The drive home is its own horror story. The first five minutes feel magical…new beginnings, puppy smell, happy passengers. Then comes the whining, the drooling, and the projectile stomach betrayal all over your lap. The puppy wiggles free of the towel, tries to crawl into the driver's seat, and howls like you're taking it to the afterlife. You juggle a coffee, the steering wheel, and a dog who just discovered motion sickness while whispering, "What have I done?" It's the first of many moments when love and regret mix in equal measure.

I always tell people the first 48 hours set the tone. Those two days are a crash course in humility. The ride home from the breeder starts cute. Puppy sleeps, you snap a picture. Then it wakes up and projectile-pees on your lap. Welcome to parenthood. By the time you get home, you're tired, the car smells like fear and disinfectant, and the dog is vibrating with joy because everything in the universe is new and edible.

The first night is chaos disguised as innocence. You put the puppy in the crate, walk away, and the wailing begins. Not a whimper. A full-body existential scream that could raise the dead. You stare at the crate, unsure if you're torturing it or saving your house. The internet says "don't give in." Your nerves say "maybe just this once." You learn fast that consistency is cheaper than therapy. If you pick that puppy up every time it cries, congratulations, you've just signed up for a lifetime of canine manipulation.

The next morning you wake up on three hours of sleep to find the puppy has somehow peed inside the crate, rolled in it, and is now joyfully smearing its victory all over your floors. You start the day mopping while it zooms through the living room like a sugar-fueled toddler, and you think, maybe coffee will help. Spoiler: it won't. Nothing helps except time, structure, and the stubbornness to outlast them.

By day two, the sleep deprivation hits like a hangover you didn't earn. You start hallucinating squeak toys. You pour milk in your coffee three times because you keep forgetting you already did it. You have conversations with the puppy that sound like hostage negotiations. Every human in the house is cranky, the puppy is thriving, and you wonder how something with baby teeth can control your entire schedule. You start to understand why every veteran Lab owner laughs darkly when you mention "puppy cuddles."

You will repeat the same routine every two hours. Outside, praise, treat, back inside, play, chaos, nap, repeat. You'll swear the puppy has a bladder the size of a peanut and a vengeful streak. It doesn't. It just doesn't know yet what the rules are. You teach those rules by being calm and boring. The calmer you are, the faster they learn. Lose your temper and you've just taught a Labrador that yelling is part of the fun.

Crate training isn't cruel. It's survival. That crate is the only thing between you and a ruined house. The trick is to make it a safe cave, not a jail cell. Feed the puppy in there, toss toys inside, let it nap with the door open. When it's time to close the door, ignore the guilt-trip whining and remember that independence is learned, not gifted. You're not punishing the dog; you're preventing future lawsuits.

The biting starts around day three. People call it "mouthing." That's cute talk for "tiny alligator attached to your arm." You'll yelp, it'll think you're playing, and suddenly you're in a live-action cartoon. The key is redirecting—give them something they're allowed to shred. Frozen washcloths, chew sticks, rubber toys. Anything that's not your skin. Labs explore the world with their mouths, and you're just collateral damage until they grow up.

Family complicates everything. Grandma thinks she's helping by sneaking food under the table. The kids think it's hilarious when the puppy steals socks. Your partner swears "he listens to me." Within a week the dog has learned five conflicting rules and zero respect. Sit down with everyone in the house and agree on commands, schedules, and consequences. If one person treats the puppy like a baby and another like a Marine recruit, you're raising a schizophrenic retriever.

Families with multiple kids take the biggest hit. One forgets to latch the crate. Another "lets him out to play" while you're in the shower. The puppy poops behind the couch, chews a shoe, and the household blames each other in an endless loop of "who was watching him?" Labradors are the great equalizer. They expose weak leadership, poor communication, and marriage cracks faster than any therapist could.

Leash training in the early days is comedy. The puppy flops, chews the leash, refuses to move, then bolts after a leaf. You'll spend weeks teaching that walking beside you is more fun than dragging you into traffic. Start early. Reward often. And remember, patience is cheaper than reconstructive surgery.

The first vet visit will test your soul. The puppy will scream like you're murdering it, the vet tech will smile like this happens every day, and you'll stand there pretending you're fine while your wallet cries quietly in your back pocket. The puppy will pee on the scale, the vet will hand you a handful of pills "just in case," and you'll leave $300 poorer but relieved that your baby alligator is medically sound. You'll also notice the staff doesn't flinch when you say "Labrador." They know what's coming.

Your house will never look the same again. Rugs become training pads. The coffee table becomes a chew buffet. Shoes disappear into the void. You'll develop a sixth sense for silence—because silence means crime. You'll celebrate small wins like "no accidents today" and "he dropped it when I asked." That's progress. Celebrate it. Then buy more paper towels, because it's temporary.

The gear pile grows fast. Crate, pen, gates, chew toys, cleaning products, training treats, leashes, collars, ID tags, vet appointments, puppy classes. Every purchase feels like prevention, until you realize prevention is just organized chaos. But you'll still buy it all, because for those brief calm moments when the puppy curls up in your lap, you'd sell your car to keep that peace.

I remember one couple calling me three days after bringing their Lab home. "He's biting the kids, barking all night, and peeing every fifteen minutes. Did we get a bad one?" No, they got a normal one. Puppies are feral toddlers with better balance. The problem isn't the dog; it's that people expect instant companionship instead of months of structure.

There will be moments when you think you made a mistake. Everyone does. You'll stand in your living room at 3 a.m., in your pajamas, puppy barking at shadows, and wonder what kind of fool signs up for this. But if you stick it out, something shifts. The chaos slows. The puppy looks at you one day with that spark of recognition—"oh, you're my person." That's when it starts to make sense.

Around week three, the exhaustion becomes routine. You know the feeding schedule, the potty cues, the warning signs before a zoomie storm. You're still tired, but now it's a rhythm. The puppy starts sitting for meals, sleeping longer, following you instead of running from you. Those first cracks of maturity appear, and suddenly you're not babysitting a hurricane—you're raising a future partner.

The hardest part is teaching yourself to parent, not pamper. Cute doesn't excuse chaos. A Lab puppy that gets away with biting, jumping, or stealing food at ten weeks will still be doing it at ten months—just heavier. You're not crushing their spirit by saying "no." You're shaping a dog that won't get surrendered for doing exactly what you allowed.

Keep your expectations human. Sleep deprivation will make you cranky, accidents will test your patience, and sometimes you'll cry over nothing. That's normal. But the moment you start thinking "he's doing it to spite me," take a breath. He's not. He's doing it because he's a Labrador, and self-control hasn't downloaded yet.

By the end of the first month, you'll start to recognize the small miracles. The first time he sits without being asked. The first night he sleeps through. The first time he runs back to you instead of away. Those are the moments that matter. They're the payoff for every destroyed towel and missed hour of sleep.

There's a special kind of relief in that first stretch of silence when the crate stays quiet all night. You wake up before dawn, convinced something's wrong. Then you see the puppy sleeping soundly, twitching paws chasing dream birds, and your brain short-circuits. You realize you've turned a corner. The beast sleeps. You might too.

There's one rule that saves sanity: supervise or confine. If you can't watch the puppy, he's in the crate or pen. Freedom is earned, not assumed. People let their guard down too soon and then act shocked when the dog eats a USB cable. It's not the dog's fault. You gave an unsupervised toddler access to power tools.

As for "puppy proofing," just accept that you're decorating for survival now. Hide the cords, pick up the laundry, block the stairs, move the trash, and pray. You'll still lose something valuable. Everyone does. But at least it'll be something replaceable and not your sanity.

There's a strange intimacy that comes from raising a Labrador. They make you earn it. You bleed, sweat, clean, train, repeat, until one day the alligator in your living room becomes a shadow at your heel. That bond doesn't come from luck; it comes from the chaos you survived together.

I tell new owners this every time: love them now, but parent them first. A Labrador puppy doesn't need endless cuddles; it needs leadership wrapped in affection. If you want a calm adult, raise one with structure, patience, and a sense of humor dark enough to survive the chewing phase.

Because here's the truth—if you do this right, those sleepless nights fade faster than you think. You'll look back one day and barely remember the puddles or the bite marks.

You'll remember the first real fetch, the way he waited for your nod before leaping into the lake, the quiet evenings when he finally collapsed beside you instead of on top of you. That's the part worth every ounce of madness.

And when a friend says they're thinking about getting a Labrador puppy, you'll smile that haunted smile all seasoned owners share. You'll say, "They're amazing dogs," and you'll mean it. But deep inside, you'll add the silent warning all of us know: you are not ready. No one ever is.

CHAPTER 7
EAT, SLEEP, SHED, REPEAT: KEEPING A LABRADOR ALIVE (AND MOSTLY INTACT)

If there's one universal truth about Labradors, it's this: they live to eat. Everything. Anything. If it fits, it's food; if it doesn't, it's still food until proven otherwise. You could feed a Lab a three-course meal and they'd still follow you to the fridge like you're harboring state secrets. Their stomachs have no shame, no brakes, and no sense of consequence.

People like to say "Labs are food-motivated," which is the polite version of "Labs are vacuum cleaners with a pulse." And the thing about living with a walking stomach is that you are the only barrier between their instincts and disaster. How you handle that bowl will decide whether your Lab thrives, waddles, or ends up with their name on a vet's weight-loss whiteboard.

When they're puppies, the hunger is adorable. Those big eyes, the little paws scratching the bowl, the pitiful whine that says "I haven't eaten in years." You'll cave. Everyone caves. But overfeeding a Labrador puppy isn't love, it's sabotage. This breed grows fast and heavy, and their joints can't keep up. Every extra pound in those early months is a tax on their hips and elbows they'll pay for later. You can either give them boundaries now or a limp later. Pick one.

Puppy feeding schedules are a balancing act between sanity and stool quality. Three small meals a day until about six months, then down to two. The food should be a high-quality puppy formula with controlled calcium and phosphorus — no, not the bag with the golden retriever on it from the grocery store, the one that costs a little more but doesn't set the stage for orthopedic hell. Feed for condition, not for the chart on the bag. Those portions are written by marketing teams, not nutritionists.

Labs don't self-regulate. They don't stop when full; they stop when physically incapable of swallowing another molecule. I've seen puppies so bloated they looked like beach balls with legs. That's not "cute." That's bloat waiting to happen. Bloat kills dogs. It's not a maybe. It's a "get to the vet now or you'll be digging a hole" situation.

So you feed small, measured amounts, you stay boringly consistent, and you never, ever "eyeball it." Measuring cups are not suggestions; they're armor. And when that puppy finishes, looks at you with betrayal in its eyes, and tries to gaslight you into a second dinner, you need to hold the line. You control the bowl, you control the chaos.

Once they hit adolescence, the metabolism changes. The Lab that used to burn calories like a hummingbird now stores them like a hoarder. The worst mistake people make is not adjusting. They keep feeding the same portions, adding treats, sneaking extras, and pretending it's "just puppy fluff." Then the vet hits you with the number on the scale and you realize your dog is fifty pounds of denial wrapped in fur.

Obesity isn't cute; it's cruel. A fat Lab is a ticking time bomb for hips, knees, heart, and pancreas. It's not about looks; it's about lifespan. Every pound over healthy weight shortens their life. I've seen dogs so heavy they can't get up without help, owners cooing "he's just big-boned" while the dog's joints scream in Morse code. Labs don't make themselves obese — we do.

Adult maintenance feeding is about portion, routine, and willpower. Feed twice a day, same time, same place. Pick a food that matches their lifestyle. A couch Lab doesn't need performance fuel, and a working Lab can't run on low-protein filler. If the food bag looks like it was designed by a CrossFit influencer, be suspicious. The "grain-free miracle diet" craze has already given us dogs with heart disease. Boutique isn't better; it's just more expensive marketing for people who shop with guilt.

Feed science, not hype. Real meat protein, healthy fats, digestible carbs, and proven formulations. You want "AAFCO tested," not "inspired by wolves." Wolves don't live long, and they definitely don't have your carpet.

Treats are currency, not meals. Use them wisely. Count them as part of the daily intake, not bonus calories. And for the love of all things holy, stop sharing human food like you're at Thanksgiving. You're not bonding, you're inflating. That one slice of pizza crust means nothing to you, but to a fifty-pound Lab it's like eating an entire cheeseburger.

If your dog starts begging, remember who trained them to. Labs are world-class manipulators. They watch routines, learn your tells, and weaponize eye contact. The moment you give in "just once," you've enrolled in a lifelong behavioral contract you'll never win. You think you're teaching kindness; they think they're teaching Pavlov.

And then there's hydration. You can offer a stainless-steel bowl of clean water, and they'll still go drink from the toilet like it's a Michelin-starred experience. It's not filth; it's novelty. You can only manage it with closed lids, frequent refills, and acceptance that Labs will forever believe everything wet is fair game.

Adult Labs thrive on routine. Same feeding time, same walk, same nap, same bowl. Change it and you'll get side-eye, sulking, or gastrointestinal revenge. They're creatures of predictable chaos, and food is their religion.

Then comes the middle age spread. Around five or six, the metabolism slows down again. They don't zoom as much, but the appetite stays prehistoric. This is when owners start saying "he's filling out." Translation: "we're both pretending he's not fat." The trick here isn't starvation; it's math. Fewer calories, more movement, more accountability. If the ribs are hidden under a layer of denial, time to adjust.

Exercise and diet work together. You can't out-walk a bad feeding plan. I've met people who jog five miles a day and still have obese Labs because they dump food "by feel." Don't guess. Measure, record, adjust. If you want data, use it. Weight charts, body condition scores, monthly weigh-ins. You don't need a spreadsheet; you need honesty.

By senior years, everything slows down. The spark's still there, but the joints creak, the naps stretch longer, and the food obsession never fades. Now it's about maintenance, not performance. Senior formulas with controlled fat, joint support, and digestibility help. Too much protein can tax the kidneys, too little leaves them weak. Ask your vet for bloodwork every year, because "he looks fine" stopped being a health metric five birthdays ago.

Older Labs have a bad habit of losing muscle and gaining padding. They don't look obese; they look "comfortable." It's the slow creep of age and kindness. We start feeding with nostalgia instead of need. You feel guilty denying them the joy of snacks when time feels shorter, but remember: keeping them lean is the kindest thing you can do. Arthritis doesn't care about sentimentality.

I once worked with a twelve-year-old Lab who could barely stand. The owner cried while telling me he "loved food too much to cut back." The dog didn't need food; he needed relief. They all do, if we'd just get out of our own way. Love isn't indulgence; it's stewardship. You decide whether they live comfortably or painfully.

Labs are also pros at hiding discomfort. They'll eat through nausea, play through soreness, wag through pain. You have to watch the subtleties: slower stairs, less enthusiasm for walks, hesitation before jumping in the car. Those are the early whispers of age. Adjust the food, trim the calories, add fish oil and glucosamine, and make their comfort the priority.

And for the love of science, skip the diet fads. "Raw food cleans teeth" is like saying cigarettes clear lungs. "Grain-free keeps coats shiny" might also keep cardiologists rich. If you want the truth, talk to a vet who knows nutrition, not an influencer with a ring light. Feed balanced, proven diets from companies that fund research, not TikTok dances.

Every few months someone asks, "What's the best food?" My answer never changes: the one your dog thrives on, not the one that makes you feel morally superior.

Feeding time isn't just about nutrition. It's ritual. It's the heartbeat of a Lab's day. That clatter of kibble is the soundtrack of devotion. You'll see the same joy at meal number three thousand as you did at meal number one. It's humbling and a little pathetic, but it's also beautiful.

The hardest part of feeding a Lab isn't choosing food; it's saying no. Saying no to the stare, the paw, the guilt. Saying no when they drop the tennis ball at your feet, not for play, but for negotiation. Saying no when you know they'll love you anyway.

I've known owners who measured meals down to the gram, and owners who free-fed out of laziness. The first produced athletes; the second produced medical bills. Balance is in the middle. Feed enough for fuel, not for silence. If your dog begs constantly, it's not hunger — it's habit. Hunger stops; habits don't.

Feeding is where control and affection collide. A Labrador's love language is food. Yours has to be discipline. You control the bowl; you control the balance. You're not denying love by limiting food; you're defining it. You're telling your dog, "I love you enough to keep you around longer."

I'll never forget my old Lab, Diesel. Food was his religion, and I was his high priest. He'd sit perfectly still, drool pooling like a waterfall, eyes locked on me with the intensity of a saint waiting for absolution. Every meal was a ceremony. And every time I said, "That's enough," he'd sigh like the world was ending, then lick the bowl clean anyway. He lived to fifteen. Lean, strong, stubborn as hell. I credit that entirely to portion control and spite.

So, feed your Labrador like you mean it — thoughtfully, precisely, consistently. Don't let guilt dictate the scoop. Don't let eyes make you weak. Don't let love turn into neglect.

Because in the end, this isn't about food. It's about trust. You hold the bowl, they hold the faith. You can make that faith keep them healthy, or you can feed it until it kills them.

The choice is yours.

Chapter 8
The Lab Owner's Medical Manual

Owning a Labrador means you'll eventually become an amateur medic whether you planned to or not. You'll learn to diagnose, clean, treat, and triage faster than most people can Google "what's this bump." It's not a matter of *if* something happens — it's *when*. Labs are tough, loyal, and catastrophically good at hurting themselves in dumb ways. They'll run full speed into a fence, eat half a towel, and look proud of it. Your job isn't to panic; it's to notice early and act fast.

The big stuff always starts small. A limp that looks cute, an ear that smells a little funky, a scratch that doesn't heal. Ignore it, and it becomes a vet bill that makes you consider crowdfunding. Every Lab owner eventually learns to spot trouble before it explodes. It's not paranoia, it's survival.

Hips: Genetics load the gun, lifestyle pulls the trigger.

Start with the hips. Everyone's heard of hip dysplasia, but most people think it's a genetic lottery ticket — either your dog gets it or doesn't. Reality's crueler. Genetics load the gun, lifestyle pulls the trigger. Letting a young Lab grow too fast, jump too early, or pack on weight is a recipe for disaster. You can't stop bad hips entirely, but you can delay the fallout. Keep puppies lean, give them traction, rugs, yoga mats, anything better than slippery tile...skip the endless stairs and high-impact fetch. Controlled exercise builds muscle that protects joints; couch potato living and weekend-warrior sprints tear them apart.

I've seen it too many times: a nine-month-old puppy limping after fetch, owner laughing it off as "too much fun." Two years later, that same dog's getting X-rays and pain meds. You can't fix dysplasia with denial. Catch it early, manage it aggressively, and you'll buy them years of mobility. Joint supplements, omega-3s, regular low-impact exercise, and honest weight control are the best insurance you can buy.

Elbows: Launch mode has a price.

The elbows are next. Labrador elbows are engineering nightmares. They bear the brunt of all that "launch into everything" energy. Dysplasia, arthritis, ligament strains — they all come from the same story: too much too soon. If your Lab limps after hard play, it's not "just sore." It's a signal. Rest them. Ice it. If it happens more than once, get films taken. The people who catch it early can manage it; the ones who wait end up scheduling surgery.

Ears: The Lab's soggy Achilles' heel.

Then there are the ears — the Achilles' heel of the breed. Those floppy, velvety ears that everyone loves are basically moisture traps. Combine trapped air, water, and the Labrador's obsession with swimming, and you've got a Petri dish that smells like old cheese and misery.

You'll know it when it hits. The dog starts shaking its head like it's trying to launch it into orbit. You catch a whiff of something foul, peek inside, and see redness, maybe brown gunk, maybe pus if you've ignored it too long. That's an ear infection. And once a Lab gets one, it's like a subscription service. They'll keep coming back until you make cleaning a religion.

Forget the fancy "all-natural" drops that smell like lavender. You need a vet-approved cleaner, a towel you don't mind ruining, and the willpower to do it weekly forever. If the infection's deep, antibiotics or antifungal meds are non-negotiable. Pretending you can "let it clear up" is like leaving a fire smoldering under your couch.

Eyes: Catch cloudiness before they crash into a wall.

Eyes come next. Labradors tend to develop cataracts, especially the yellows. You'll first notice a cloudy look, maybe a hesitation at night or reluctance on stairs. Don't wait for them to walk into a wall. Eye problems move fast. Catch them early and you can slow the damage with meds or surgery. Ignore them, and you'll be explaining to house guests why your "healthy" eight-year-old now uses sound instead of sight.

Skin: Allergies, hot spots, and despair.

Skin issues? Where do we even start. Labs collect allergies the way toddlers collect bruises. Grass, pollen, dust mites, food , it's all fair game. You'll see the signs: licking paws, red bellies, raw patches, endless scratching. Then come the hot spots, those nasty wet wounds that appear overnight. They spread fast, stink worse, and make your dog miserable.

Step one: trim the hair around it, clean it with diluted chlorhexidine, dry it, and for the love of hygiene, stop them from licking it. Cone of shame, wrap, distraction; whatever it takes. Then figure out *why* it happened. Allergies? Fleas? Moisture under the collar? A Lab's skin doesn't just "act up" for no reason. There's always a trigger. You find it or you keep treating symptoms until your wallet cries.

And speaking of fleas, if you're still "not a fan of chemicals," congratulations…you've just declared war with no armor. Preventatives exist for a reason. Same with ticks and heartworm. Every year I meet someone who "didn't think their dog needed it." Then they're standing at the vet, crying, because their pet's heartworm positive or covered in Lyme-induced arthritis. Fleas, ticks, and mosquitos don't care about your opinions. They'll ruin your dog whether you believe in medicine or not.

Dental health sounds minor until you realize how many dogs die from infections that start in their mouths. Labs love to chew but rarely on the stuff that actually cleans their teeth. Kibble isn't dental care, no matter what the bag says. Get the toothbrush. Use it. Chews help, but not enough. A vet cleaning every couple of years keeps bacteria from turning your dog's mouth into a biological weapon.

And then there's the nuclear threat: bloat. It doesn't happen every day, but when it does, it's catastrophic. The stomach fills with gas, twists, and traps blood flow. You'll see the signs; drooling, swollen belly, pacing, vomiting that produces nothing, restlessness. You've got minutes, not hours. That's a straight-to-the-emergency-clinic situation, no hesitation. It's surgical or fatal. Feed smaller meals, use slow bowls, avoid exercise right after eating, and know the signs like your life depends on it, because your dog's does.

You'll also learn that Labs have a talent for growing lumps. Cysts, lipomas, benign tumors — they sprout them like weeds. Ninety percent are harmless, but you can't tell which ten percent aren't without a needle. The rule is simple: if it's new, growing, changing, or bothering the dog, get it checked. Waiting for "next month" is how small problems become eulogies.

Every Lab owner will face the 2 a.m. panic moment, the weird cough, the limp that wasn't there earlier, the random swelling, the "oh god what is that on his belly." You'll type symptoms into Google and diagnose him with six terminal illnesses and a demon possession. Breathe. If it's not bleeding, seizing, or bloating, you can usually wait until morning. If you're not sure, call an emergency vet. They exist for exactly this reason.

Preventive care is the difference between surviving and paying for your own stupidity. Vaccines are not a suggestion. Parvo, distemper, and leptospirosis are real and they're killers. Don't skip boosters because "he never leaves the yard." Disease doesn't care about fences.

The same goes for annual bloodwork and senior checkups. Catching kidney disease or thyroid imbalance early can add years. Skip it, and you'll be blindsided when your "perfectly healthy" dog collapses out of nowhere.

Insurance isn't a luxury, it's a necessity. I've seen people sell furniture to cover ACL repairs and GoFundMe their way through cancer treatments. Pet insurance keeps you from choosing between your dog and your rent. It's what keeps 'I love him' from turning into 'I had no choice.' Pick a plan that covers accidents and illness, not just wellness visits. Read the fine print, file your claims, and don't assume love pays bills.

The thing about Labradors is they hide pain. It's in their DNA to push through, keep playing, keep wagging. By the time they limp, cry, or stop eating, it's serious. You have to read the whispers…a slight hitch in the gait, extra licking on one paw, a missed jump onto the couch. They'll never tell you outright. You've got to listen harder than most people care to.

I remember a client who called about her seven-year-old Lab "acting off." Eating less, not running as much. She waited two weeks before coming in. The diagnosis was splenic cancer. We caught it too late. She'd been waiting for something obvious. Labs never show obvious. They just fade.

The key to keeping them healthy isn't perfection; it's consistency. Clean the ears, brush the teeth, check the skin, feel the joints, note the weird stuff. Make it routine, not panic-driven. The people who pay attention catch things when they're fixable. The ones who don't end up writing long Facebook posts about "how it happened so fast."

Your job isn't to bubble-wrap your dog; it's to stay alert and act early. You can't prevent genetics, but you can manage outcomes. Keep them lean, keep them clean, keep them moving, and listen to your gut. It's usually right.

Labs are resilient to a fault. They'll keep running on torn ligaments, keep swimming with ear infections, keep wagging with abscesses. They're built from loyalty and denial. So it's on you to be the adult in the room — the one who says "enough."

The best owners I've known weren't rich, but they were observant. They noticed things, asked questions, and didn't wait. They didn't freak out, they didn't Google themselves into hysteria, they just took responsibility. That's all medicine really is, paying attention and doing something before it's too late.

You'll save yourself heartache and your Lab a world of pain by remembering one simple rule: early beats heroic. Every time.

So, when your dog starts shaking his head, scratching his ear, limping after fetch, or staring off like something's wrong, don't scroll the forums. Check, clean, call, act. Prevention isn't glamorous, but it's what keeps a Labrador's body running like the machine it was built to be.

In the end, being your dog's health advocate isn't about avoiding vet bills. It's about earning the years you'll get together. Responsibility is the best medicine, and awareness is the cure for most of the heartbreak people call "bad luck."

If you do your job right, your Lab will live a long, loud, filthy, happy life and you'll have the scars, the receipts, and the peace of mind to prove it.

LABRADOR RETRIEVER INSIGHTS

CHAPTER 9
SHORT HAIR, BIG LIE: GROOMING THE LABRADOR DISASTER ZONE

People love to say Labradors are "low maintenance" because they're short-haired. That phrase has probably caused more heartbreak than bad breeders and expired kibble combined. The coat may look tidy, but it sheds like a snow globe filled with static. You don't own a Lab—you share square footage with one continuous cloud of fur. It's in your coffee, your keyboard, your bra, and occasionally your dinner. If you ever wondered what it's like to live inside a lint trap, congratulations, you're about to find out.

You can't stop the shedding. You can only surrender to it. Twice a year they blow coat so aggressively you start questioning the laws of biology. How can a dog still have hair after that much came off? I've filled garbage bags. I've watched tumbleweeds of undercoat drift across the floor like ghost puppies. And every spring and fall, I think, "This time maybe it won't be so bad." Then my vacuum screams for mercy and the carpet changes color.

The trick is routine. A quick brush every day beats a war every weekend. The right tools matter: a slicker brush for surface fluff, a deshedding rake for the dense stuff, a rubber curry for bath time. The Furminator isn't magic—it's just the only thing standing between you and insanity. Use it gently, work in small sections, and accept that you'll still find fur on your toast.

Labs have double coats: a dense undercoat for insulation and a topcoat that sheds water and your will to live. That's what kept their ancestors alive in freezing North Atlantic water and what keeps your house looking like a crime scene made of fluff. The undercoat cycles constantly; it's why you can brush for an hour and still pull out enough hair to build a new dog. Brush until you think you're done, then brush again. You're never done.

Bathing a Lab is a full-contact sport. You'll start with good intentions—warm water, gentle shampoo, towels lined up like you're running a spa. Two minutes later, there's water on the ceiling, shampoo in your eyes, and the dog's shaking hard enough to register on seismographs. Labs see baths as punishment for crimes they haven't committed. Still, you need to bathe them every couple of months or when they smell like dead fish and regret. Use a mild dog shampoo, rinse like your reputation depends on it, and for the love of your plumbing, towel them dry before they bolt for the couch.

And that's when it happens—the post-bath chaos. You'll spend thirty minutes bathing them, another twenty trying to dry them, and then release a freshly cleaned maniac back into your house. They'll sprint through the halls like they've just escaped prison, slam into furniture, roll on every rug, and somehow find the one patch of dirt you missed in the yard. You'll stand there dripping and swearing while your Lab joyfully re-baptizes itself in mud. Somewhere between the third shake-off and the couch collision, you'll accept that "clean" is only a temporary illusion.

A good microfiber towel is worth its weight in gold. Better yet, two. Labs can soak through one before you blink. Skip the hairdryer unless you enjoy the scent of wet-dog steam. Let them air dry somewhere that isn't your bed. If you have a yard, let the sun do the work while they roll in dirt and undo everything you just accomplished.

Then comes the smell. Wet dog isn't just an odor—it's an atmosphere. You can light candles, burn sage, or buy every "fresh meadow" spray on the shelf; it won't help. The only cure is clean water, regular brushing, and a healthy sense of humor. The smell means your Lab's doing exactly what it was built to do: repel water, trap odor, and ruin upholstery.

Ear care is next on the list of necessary torture. Every Lab owner eventually learns that floppy ears are basically mold incubators. Water gets trapped after every swim or bath, and if you don't dry them, you'll be visiting the vet for infections that smell like a cheese factory in August. A cotton ball and vet-approved cleaner once a week saves you hundreds of dollars and your dog endless head-shaking.

Just pour the cleaner in, massage the base, let them shake out the gunk, and pretend you're not getting sprayed.

Nail trimming is another adventure. Most Labs act like you're sawing off limbs when you so much as touch their paws. The trick is frequency and bribery. Do it often, start early, and use good clippers. If you let nails grow long, they change the way the dog walks and mess up joints. Trim little bits often instead of big chunks rarely. If you hear clicking on the floor, you've waited too long.

Dental care's the most ignored part of maintenance and the most important. That "dog breath" people joke about isn't normal—it's infection. Brushing teeth three times a week keeps plaque from turning into vet bills. Use dog toothpaste; human stuff can kill them. If brushing's a war, dental wipes or enzymatic chews help, but nothing beats a brush and a little backbone. Your dog's mouth shouldn't smell like roadkill.

You'll also learn that Labs have a special relationship with mud. They don't just get dirty—they become art installations. Give them five minutes in a clean yard and they'll find the one patch of sludge left from last winter. Rinse, towel, repeat. Dirt is their love language. It's also why you should keep a "dog towel" by every door and lower your housekeeping standards to survival mode.

I used to think I could win against the hair. I bought lint rollers in bulk, vacuumed daily, even wore black like it was a protest statement. Then one morning I found a single blonde hair in my coffee at work—three miles from home—and realized the truth. You don't beat the fur. You coexist with it. Once you accept that, grooming stops feeling like punishment and starts feeling like meditation.

You brush, they sigh, the world gets quiet for a minute. It's the only time a Labrador holds still and looks half-angelic. Their eyes close, their breathing slows, and for a brief moment you forget they just shed enough to fill a pillow. Grooming becomes therapy—for you and them. It's connection disguised as maintenance. Because grooming was never just maintenance. It was therapy in disguise. For both of you.

Seasonal shedding teaches humility. You can vacuum, sweep, brush, and still lose the war. But every hair in that pile tells a story: every swim, every nap, every zoomie through a field. It's the physical proof of a life lived loud. You'll curse it, but one day when they're gone, you'll find one stubborn hair stuck in your sweater and it'll gut you. That's the paradox of Labs: the mess is the memory.

For newcomers, here's reality. Groom once a week in the off-season, three or four times during heavy shed. Clean ears weekly, trim nails every two weeks, brush teeth often enough to feel like a dentist, and bathe every couple of months. That's the minimum if you want a clean dog and a livable house. Anything less, and you're living in a fur-based ecosystem.

Buy good tools. Cheap brushes break, dull clippers split nails, bad towels breed mildew. Quality pays for itself when you're not constantly replacing stuff. And invest in a decent vacuum with a pet-hair attachment. Not because it'll fix the problem, but because it'll help you pretend you still have control.

You'll get used to scheduling life around grooming. Want to wear black? Brush first. Hosting guests? Vacuum twice and surrender. Laundry day? Check the lint trap before it catches fire. Grooming isn't about vanity—it's survival.

And then there's the graveyard of gadgets. Every Lab owner eventually falls for the miracle tools—the gloves that "lift hair effortlessly," the self-cleaning brushes that jam after two uses, the trendy dryers that sound like jet engines. You'll try them all. Half will break, the other half will just move fur from one surface to another. The only miracle tool that's never failed me is a decent broom and low expectations.

There's also something grounding about it. You can't scroll your phone while brushing a Lab. You can't fake patience with a creature that hates the hair dryer but loves rolling in dead things. Grooming forces you to slow down, focus, and laugh at the absurdity of living with a four-legged shedding machine that still thinks it's clean.

Somewhere along the way, you stop caring about fur on furniture and start measuring success by how fast you can clean ears without losing an eye. You start bragging about the softness of your dog's coat like you had anything to do with it. You learn to time baths around your own schedule and the weather forecast, and you stop apologizing when

66

people leave your house covered in hair. It's a lifestyle, not a mess.

After a good session, when the last brushstroke's done and the air smells faintly of shampoo and wet optimism, there's this pause. Your Lab leans into you, half-asleep, trusting you completely. You're covered in fur, the floor's a disaster, and somehow you've never felt calmer. That's the real reward. Not the clean dog, but the quiet moment after—the heartbeat of routine and love that makes all the hair worth it.

Labs will never be tidy, but they'll always be worth it. You'll come to recognize the smell of clean fur, the feel of brushed coat under your hand, the rhythmic sound of them breathing while you work. You'll catch yourself talking to them mid-bath, threatening to trade them for a goldfish, while they stare up at you like you hung the moon.

That's the real secret. Grooming isn't about making them perfect; it's about keeping them healthy and keeping yourself sane. The hair, the smell, the constant need—it's the price of admission for a relationship built on mud, drool, and devotion.

So brush the dog. Vacuum the floor. Light the candle. Then pour a drink and toast to the truth: you'll never win the war on fur, but you'll always love the soldier who started it.

CHAPTER 10
THE LABRADOR BRAIN: THEY DON'T OBEY YOU, THEY NEGOTIATE

The first thing you need to know about training a Labrador is this: they're not dumb. They just think *you* are. Every single one of them walks into your house assuming they're middle management and you're the intern. You can almost see it in their eyes—"Ah, excellent, a new human assistant. Let's get this operation running."

People love to brag about how smart Labs are. That's the problem. Intelligence without boundaries is just mischief in a hoodie. These dogs read tone, posture, and mood faster than a therapist on espresso. They know when you're bluffing, when you're mad, and when they can push the limit. They don't "obey" you out of devotion. They negotiate. You're not teaching commands; you're brokering treaties.

That's why the "eager to please" myth drives me insane. Labs aren't trying to please you—they're trying to *please themselves* without losing access to snacks. Their brains run on a simple operating system: food, play, chaos, repeat. If pleasing you fits into that cycle, lucky you. If it doesn't, prepare to be ignored.

The real art of training a Labrador isn't dominance; it's psychology. You're shaping behavior while outsmarting a creature whose emotional intelligence rivals a toddler with a sugar problem. The difference is the toddler can't jump the fence or eat drywall.

Positive reinforcement works—if you actually understand what it means. It's not endless treats for existing. It's timing, consistency, and clarity. Reinforce what you want, ignore or redirect what you don't, and quit thinking "no" is a training plan. Labs crave structure. Without it, they become self-employed. And a self-employed Lab is the CEO of destruction.

Crate training gets a bad reputation because people treat it like punishment. It's not jail. It's a seatbelt. Done right, it's where the dog learns impulse control, patience, and how to exist without you hovering. Labs are Velcro with teeth—they bond hard and fast, and then panic when you vanish for ten minutes. The crate teaches them solitude without meltdown. Start slow, make it positive, and resist the urge to comfort every whine. They're manipulating you. They do that.

I've had owners swear their dog "hates the crate" while the Lab inside looks perfectly fine, quietly testing how many seconds of whining it takes to make the human cave. That's not fear. That's research. And congratulations, you're the lab rat.

Impulse control is the hill most owners die on. These dogs act first, consider later, and apologize never. A Lab's brain is wired for motion—chasing, grabbing, eating, repeating. Training impulse control is teaching a sprinting engine to idle. It takes time, boredom, and a complete absence of human ego.

Start with "sit" and "stay," not because they're flashy, but because they're grounding. They're the off switch. Once a Lab understands that calm earns reward, the chaos gets manageable. But if you reward excitement—throwing the ball when they're screaming, feeding when they're bouncing—you've just taught hyperactivity as a skill.

And that brings us to one of the biggest myths in the dog world: that you can "exercise away" bad behavior. You can't run the crazy out of a Lab. You can only teach it to think before it detonates. Physical fatigue isn't the same as mental balance. I've met owners who jogged their Labs five miles a day, then came home to shredded couches because the dog's body was tired but its brain was starving. Mental enrichment—training drills, puzzles, scent work—burns energy in ways miles never will. Without that outlet, the smartest breed in the room becomes the most destructive.

Consistency beats intensity. People love one-day miracles, but Labs need patterns. They learn faster from daily five-minute sessions than from one exhausting boot camp weekend. Keep cues simple, tone calm, and expectations realistic. You're building habits, not training circus tricks.

Recall is where the gods of obedience go to die. You'll call, they'll look, and then sprint in the opposite direction like you just declared freedom. The key to recall is value. You have to be more interesting than the world. Food helps, but enthusiasm matters more. Call like you mean it, reward like it's Vegas, and never—ever—chase them. The moment you chase, it's a game. And you will lose.

I once spent forty minutes trying to catch a Lab named Benny who'd stolen a loaf of bread. Every time I got close, he wagged, grinned, and sprinted just out of reach. I finally sat down on the ground. He came trotting over like, "Hey, you okay?" That's the Labrador brain in action—smart enough to win, sweet enough to check on you, and shameless enough to steal again tomorrow.

Then comes the adolescent phase, the time when even well-trained Labs decide to lose their damn minds. Somewhere between seven months and a year and a half, their brains melt. They forget everything you ever taught them, stop listening, and develop selective hearing that could rival a teenager's. It's not rebellion; it's biology. Hormones, growth, independence—all hitting at once. This is the phase when owners panic, declare their dog "untrainable," and start Googling rescues. Don't. Ride it out, stay consistent, and keep training. The brain comes back online eventually, and all the work you thought was wasted will kick in like muscle memory.

Training isn't about domination; it's communication. You're teaching another species to decode your signals and respond with cooperation instead of chaos. The leash isn't control—it's translation. Pull too hard and they fight. Stay calm, and they sync up. Half the people who complain their Labs "don't listen" are just yelling in a language the dog doesn't understand.

The food obsession helps and hurts. Yes, you can teach a Lab anything with snacks. But if you overdo it, they'll hold out for better pay. Labs are master negotiators. The moment you hand over a treat for mediocre effort, they log it as policy. Use variable rewards: sometimes a treat, sometimes a toy, sometimes pure praise. Keep them guessing, and they'll keep working.

People confuse positive reinforcement with permissive chaos. Letting your Lab jump on everyone, mouth hands, or ignore commands because "he's just excited" isn't kindness. It's neglect disguised as affection. You wouldn't let a toddler swing a baseball bat in the living room; don't let your dog practice bad behavior and call it love.

Mental stimulation is as important as physical. A tired Lab isn't just one that ran six miles—it's one that used its brain. Scent work, puzzle toys, hide-and-seek, structured fetch. Give them purpose or they'll invent one, and you won't like it. I've seen Labs train themselves to open refrigerators, unzip backpacks, and dismantle baby gates just to see if they could. Spoiler: they could.

And here's the hard truth from twenty years in the trenches: most "bad" Labs aren't bad dogs. They're victims of human inconsistency. Training fails when people lose their patience, change the rules daily, or take disobedience personally. You're not raising a furry child who "knows better." You're teaching a creature that lives entirely in the moment. If your timing sucks, your communication's sloppy, or your emotions get loud, they're just reacting to that. The dog isn't challenging your authority—it's waiting for you to get your act together.

If you're losing your mind, that's normal. Training a Lab tests patience like nothing else. You'll question your methods, your sanity, and occasionally your life choices. The important part is not quitting when it gets messy. Progress with this breed is measured in half-victories: the first loose-leash walk that doesn't feel like a CrossFit session, the first sit at the door instead of a body slam, the first recall that actually works when it counts.

Some people reach a breaking point and call in a trainer. That's not weakness; that's wisdom. A good trainer isn't there to fix your dog—they're there to fix your communication. If your Lab ignores you, odds are you're speaking gibberish. Professionals translate. And they do it without the emotional baggage of ownership.

Labs learn what gets them what they want. If chaos earns attention, they'll choose chaos every time. Ignore bad behavior, reward calm, and control your reactions. Every sigh, every flinch, every shout teaches them something. You're always training—whether you mean to or not.

There's a moment in every owner's life when they realize their Lab has trained *them*. You'll start pre-measuring meals so they don't bark, adjusting your schedule around their zoomies, spelling out "walk" to avoid premature explosions. That's not failure—it's adaptation. You live with intelligence; you bend or break.

Labs don't think in good and evil. They think in outcomes. Behavior that pays off repeats. It's that simple and that ruthless. The faster you stop personalizing it, the faster you'll succeed. Your dog isn't defying you out of spite; it's just running experiments on reinforcement theory.

Over time, you'll notice something shift. The chaos starts to sync with rhythm. The jumping fades, the leash goes slack, the recall sticks. You'll start trusting each other. That's when training stops feeling like control and starts feeling like conversation. You're not yelling; you're speaking fluently.

The myth of perfection ruins good dogs. Labs don't need to be flawless; they need to be functional. They need direction, patience, and humor. A well-trained Lab isn't robotic—it's confident, connected, and just a little mischievous. You want obedience that breathes, not obedience that breaks.

I've worked Labs that could ace a field trial one minute and eat a sandwich off a picnic table the next. That's not failure. That's the breed. They live big, love hard, and screw up spectacularly. Training them is about learning to laugh while holding a leash.

There will be days when you swear your dog's possessed. There will be nights when you question every decision that led you here. But there will also be mornings when your Lab heels perfectly through chaos, looks up at you with that stupid, perfect grin, and you realize you're both doing the best you can.

The Labrador brain is a beautiful mess—equal parts loyalty, greed, and mischief. You can't crush it into obedience; you can only guide it toward sanity. Train with food, patience, and humor, and you'll end up with a partner who chooses to listen instead of obeys from fear.

Training doesn't end when they "know the commands." It never ends. It evolves. The old cues turn into muscle memory, new challenges appear, and the relationship deepens. The goal isn't perfection; it's trust. It's being able to walk into any chaos, leash in hand, and know you'll both come out the other side in one piece.

At the end of it all, remember this: you're not training a dog, you're building a dialogue with a creature that loves you too much to make it easy. Train like you're teaching a toddler with teeth. Laugh more than you yell. And when they finally get it right, don't just reward them—thank them for letting you be part of their ridiculous, wonderful chaos.

Chapter 11
Chaos Management 101: How to Outthink a Labrador (Good Luck)

Living with a Labrador means living in a constant state of mild disaster. You don't "train out" the chaos—you just learn to direct it toward things that don't cost as much. They're not bad dogs. They're creative engineers with anxiety and jaws of steel. Everything they do—chewing, digging, stealing, jumping, garbage raids—has logic behind it. The problem is that their logic is prehistoric, and yours is based on carpet cleaning and rent deposits.

Chewing comes first. It always does. Puppies chew because their mouths hurt, adults chew because they're bored, and seniors chew because nostalgia's a hell of a drug. The day you bring a Lab home, it's only a matter of time before they find the one thing you can't replace and make it into modern art. You'll walk into a room and see fluff snowing from a couch cushion or the mangled remains of your headphones, and they'll greet you like, "Look! Enrichment!"

People call it "bad behavior." It's not. It's instinct and opportunity. A Lab with nothing to do will chew something just to see what happens. That's how they learn. Their ancestors dragged nets through icy water for twelve hours a day; yours has been left alone with Amazon boxes. You can't expect evolution to keep up with your Wi-Fi.

The solution isn't punishment—it's preparation. Rotate safe chews like you're managing a toddler toy library. Freeze wet food in Kongs, stuff marrow bones, hide treats in puzzle feeders. Give them something they can destroy on purpose. If you don't, they'll choose for you, and your remote control will die a martyr.

Then comes counter-surfing, the Olympic event of Labrador sin. You think you've put food far enough back. You haven't. They'll stretch, balance, and snatch a loaf of bread with the precision of a jewel thief. Once they learn a counter produces snacks, you've created a lifelong scavenger. This isn't hunger—it's performance art.

The fix is management and vigilance. Don't leave temptation out. Teach "leave it" like your sanity depends on it, because it does. Reward them when they ignore bait, and stop believing they "know better." They don't. They know physics.

Jumping is another masterpiece of misplaced affection. Labs don't jump to dominate; they jump because they're spring-loaded happiness grenades. Every fiber of their being screams "Hi! Hi! Hi!" and your ribs are just collateral damage. You can't extinguish joy—you have to redirect it. Teach four paws on the ground gets attention; jumping gets ignored. Consistency from every human in the house is non-negotiable. One soft-hearted guest undoing your work equals another month of flying-dog hugs.

Stealing, or as Labs call it, "interactive possession," is part mischief, part intelligence test. They grab socks, remotes, or underwear not to eat them (well, not always) but because it gets you moving. It's fetch, but you're the toy. Chasing a thief reinforces the theft, so don't. Trade up instead: "Drop" followed by a jackpot reward. Convince them surrendering loot is profitable. Outwit them, don't out-yell them.

Digging follows the same rule. It's never random. They dig to cool down, bury treasures, or relieve stress. If your yard looks like a moon landing site, give them a designated dig zone. Sandpit, soft dirt, buried toys—problem solved. Labs love rules when they make sense. Give them permission to misbehave strategically and they'll actually listen.

Garbage raids are a whole other religion. The trash can is their personal casino: sometimes you hit the jackpot, sometimes you get yelled at, but the thrill keeps them coming back. A locking lid or hidden bin ends the heist. Scolding after the fact does nothing; you're just providing dramatic feedback for next time. Prevention beats punishment every time.

Every destructive act traces back to one thing: unmet need. Labs are chaos engines powered by boredom. Walks aren't enough. They need jobs. Training drills, retrieval games, sniffing exercises—anything that activates their brain before their teeth do. Ten minutes of scent work equals an hour of peace. You want calm? Earn it.

And while we're here, let's talk about your behavior. Most owners teach destruction without realizing it. They yell when the dog grabs something, chase it around, then clean up while the Lab watches the show. That's reinforcement— negative for you, positive for them. You've turned discipline into entertainment. Dogs don't need drama. They need information. "No" means nothing unless followed by "do this instead." Replace, redirect, reward. Every. Damn. Time.

Some Labs act out because they can't handle separation. You leave, they panic, and the furniture pays. It's not vengeance—it's fear. Build tolerance slowly. Crate time, short departures, calm returns. Stop making goodbyes emotional and hellos hysterical. You're not starring in a reunion movie. Treat comings and goings like background noise, and your house survives.

I once worked with a Lab named Luna who could open cabinets, flip lids, and operate a foot pedal trash can. Her owners swore she was possessed. She wasn't. She was bored. We replaced the bin, added food puzzles, and started daily scent games. Within a week, the "demon" was just a tired, happy genius with nothing left to prove. That's most Labs: too smart, not evil.

If you've ever caught your dog mid-crime—mouth full of contraband, tail wagging—you know the guilt face. It's adorable and meaningless. They're not remorseful. They're reading your reaction and hoping to de-escalate. You're emotional; they're strategic. Next time, skip the lecture. Confiscate, clean, and move on. Save your words for when they can earn them.

You can't logic away destruction, but you can manage it. Baby gates, crates, leashes indoors, structured play—all are tools, not punishments. Structure doesn't crush a Lab's spirit; it saves it. Boundaries make them feel safe, not restricted. Think of it as creative containment. You don't remove chaos, you curate it.

And every Lab owner eventually hits burnout. That moment where you're sitting on the floor, surrounded by fur and shredded bills, wondering what fresh hell you've invited into your home. You're not broken—you're tired. You've been negotiating with a toddler in a dog suit for months. That exhaustion is part of the process. Labs push you to your limit because that's where growth lives—for both species. The trick isn't to break them or yourself; it's to build a rhythm between their madness and your expectations.

Public behavior adds another layer of shame.

The Lab who behaves like a saint indoors turns into a one-dog parade at the park.

They'll yank your arm out chasing birds, roll in mystery filth, and leap onto strangers like long-lost cousins.

Embarrassing? Absolutely. But normal.

Labs don't care about your reputation; they care about whatever smells like chicken. The only cure is exposure. Train in public. Let them fail. Reward recovery, not perfection. The world's their classroom—don't skip the field trips because you're mortified.

Enrichment is your secret weapon. Not the Pinterest version—real, practical, daily brain work. Hide treats in cardboard boxes. Scatter kibble in the grass and make them forage. Teach them to find hidden toys by scent. Use their brain so their body doesn't riot. Rotate toys weekly so novelty stays fresh. Labs thrive on purpose. You're not "spoiling" them by making them work; you're keeping them sane. A bored Lab destroys; a busy Lab naps.

And let's be honest: we humans are hypocrites. We call them hyper while we scroll on our phones for hours. We label them needy while they stare at us, waiting for direction. We brought home a working dog, then gave it a couch and a guilt complex. Labs don't fail people. People fail Labs by underestimating what they are: athletes, thinkers, and emotional barometers rolled into one slobbery package.

Owners always ask, "When does it stop?" The truth: never completely. The intensity fades, the intelligence doesn't. A well-trained Lab will still test limits, just with better manners. You'll graduate from shredded shoes to stolen sandwiches. Progress, not perfection.

The trick is perspective. Chewing, stealing, and digging aren't moral failings; they're communication. "I'm bored." "I'm anxious." "I'm curious." You either answer those messages or live in denial. The dog's not asking for dominance battles or fancy gadgets...just engagement and clarity.

When you hit your limit, and you will, remember that chaos isn't defiance. It's energy without direction. You can scream, or you can channel it. A tired, mentally satisfied Lab doesn't destroy. It naps. The destructive ones are the ones left guessing.

I've had my share of "What the hell" moments. One of my dogs once ate an entire roll of paper towels, then threw up a papier-mâché sculpture of his own regrets. I didn't punish him. I fixed my mistake. I left the opportunity. You don't fix chaos with anger; you fix it with prevention and patience.

Labs push buttons because that's how they learn where the limits are. Every chewed shoe, every counter theft, every garbage dive—it's feedback. They're mapping your reactions. The calmer and clearer you are, the faster they adapt. Lose your temper, and you just teach noise.

So, the next time you walk into a room that looks like a crime scene and your Lab greets you with a sock in its mouth and a grin that says "worth it," breathe. You're not losing the war; you're living the job description.

The goal isn't to stop the behavior—it's to outsmart it. Be smarter than the thief, faster than the jumper, and calmer than the chaos. That's how you win.

And when you finally sit down, vacuum in hand, surrounded by fur and half-chewed toys, you'll realize something: all this destruction, all this noise, it's just the soundtrack of a life shared with something that refuses to be boring.

Because a quiet Labrador is either sleeping—or plotting. And honestly, you wouldn't have it any other way.

CHAPTER 12
CHANNELING THE MADNESS
GIVING THE CHAOS A JOB

If you think exercise means a walk around the block, congratulations—you've just raised a Labrador that's ten minutes from eating drywall. These dogs weren't bred to chill; they were built to do. They need jobs like you need caffeine and Wi-Fi. Every problem this breed has—chewing, barking, anxiety, chaos—boils down to one thing: too much horsepower, nowhere to run it.

You can't train the madness out of a Lab. You can only channel it. A busy Lab is a happy Lab. A tired Lab is a peaceful Lab. And a peaceful Lab is the only kind that won't remodel your house with its teeth.

People brag, "I take my Lab for long walks." Cute. So did the fishermen of Newfoundland—only theirs were through freezing surf while dragging nets of cod. Your latte stroll doesn't scratch that itch. These dogs were engineered for labor, not leisure. The trick is giving that labor a modern shape that doesn't involve hauling fish.

Hunting is the purest form of what they were made for. Even if you never fire a gun, that instinct to locate, retrieve, and carry is sacred to them. Watching a Lab on a retrieve is like watching history move: eyes sharp, muscles wired, tail beating time with centuries of breeding. You can honor it in simple ways—training backyard bumpers, frozen birds, or water retrieves. The point isn't killing anything; it's letting that brain do what it was built to do: work with you, for you, with purpose.

If hunting isn't your thing, welcome to dock diving—Labrador heaven. It's chaos on a scoreboard: full-speed sprint, airborne launch, perfect splash. They hit the water like furry torpedoes and come up grinning. Every jump burns energy and builds focus, and it's the one sport guaranteed to send your Lab home tired instead of just wetter.

Scent work might not look impressive until you realize you're watching a biological marvel. These dogs can smell a thought. Give them boxes, cotton balls, essential oils, whatever, and let them hunt. Ten minutes of nose work will exhaust a Lab faster than an hour of fetch. It's pride disguised as sniffing. You'll see that tail wag when they nail it; that's purpose flickering back to life.

Obedience and rally work sound boring until you understand what's happening: impulse control dressed as sport. Every sit, heel, and turn forces them to think before they move, which, for a Lab, is the holy grail. It's how you turn a creature ruled by enthusiasm into one guided by partnership. The payoff isn't ribbons—it's sanity.

Agility is the wild side of that partnership. Forget the graceful Border Collies; a Lab on an agility course is a joyful wrecking ball. They crash tunnels, flatten weave poles, and look like a linebacker in a tutu—but they adore it. Agility is fast thinking in motion, teamwork in chaos. You'll both walk off the field smiling and muddy, which is the only win that matters.

Flyball? Pure speed therapy. Picture a Lab tearing down a lane, hurdling jumps, slamming a box to release a ball, and blasting back like their tail's on fire. It's loud, ridiculous, and perfect. They live for it because it gives them permission to go full throttle with rules attached.

And here's the truth: you don't need fancy sports to give your Lab a job. Structured fetch, puzzle toys, trick training, hide-and-seek in your living room—those are micro-jobs. Five minutes here and there keeps that big brain humming in the right direction. Fetch with rules: sit before the throw, wait for release, return, drop, repeat. It's obedience camouflaged as play. You'll watch confidence bloom where frustration used to live.

People claim their Labs never get tired. Wrong—they never get *fulfilled*. A two-hour walk without engagement does nothing; twenty minutes of problem-solving does everything. You can't out-walk genetics; you have to outsmart it. Training isn't about exhaustion; it's about meaning.

And I get it—you're tired. You work, you commute, you clean fur off everything you own. Then some sarcastic trainer tells you to run field drills at sunset. Fine. Make it simple. Hide kibble in muffin tins. Scatter treats under cups. Use the stairs for "up" and "down." Labs don't need fancy; they need effort that says, "I see you. Let's work."

Everyone has ten minutes. Ten minutes of engagement beats an hour of regret after your dog eats a remote. You don't need to be a professional handler; you just need to start. Stop scrolling. Throw the ball. The dog doesn't care about your excuses; it cares that you tried.

And if you swear your Lab "isn't into that stuff," you're lying. There's no such thing as a lazy Labrador, only a disengaged one. The couch potato act isn't contentment.. .it's defeat. Light that spark again and watch the reboot: sharper eyes, faster responses, real joy. I've seen it happen more times than I can count.

There was Paul, a retired guy whose Lab, Daisy, was wrecking his nerves. Loud, wild, relentless. We started scent work—cheap, easy, no props. Three weeks later Daisy was calmer than most therapy dogs. Her brain finally had a purpose. Paul stopped day-drinking. Everyone won.

That's the quiet miracle: sports and work save dogs, but they save people too. Frustration turns to laughter; guilt turns to pride. I've watched owners ready to rehome their dogs transform into teams that actually *like* each other. The Lab doesn't change...you do.

And if guilt's been chewing on you for not doing enough, here's your pardon. You're not a bad owner; you're just human. We all start with the stupid belief that love fixes everything. Then the Lab chews your car's seatbelt and you learn affection isn't a substitute for purpose. Use the guilt as fuel. The best owners aren't flawless—they're relentless. They show up again tomorrow.

You don't fix chaos with shame. You fix it with motion. It's never too late. Whether your Lab's ten weeks or ten years, fulfillment beats frustration every time. Give them something to do, and they'll forgive every mistake you've ever made.

Forget the myth that sports cost a fortune. You can build 90 percent of what you need with a ball, a kiddie pool, and imagination. Backyard drills, scent walks, cardboard puzzles. Labs don't care about your budget; they care about your effort.

Mental work isn't optional; it's survival. Without it, their brains eat themselves. People say, "He just needs to calm down." No—he needs to *do* something. A Labrador without a job is a demolition expert waiting for orders.

The more you train, the easier life gets. The leash slackens. The jumping fades. The chewing slows. Because they finally have a reason. You've turned confusion into clarity, energy into partnership. You've stopped fighting the current and started swimming with it.

Even five minutes a day changes everything. Call it the Five-Minute Fetch Hack. Structure a quick retrieve with obedience built in—sit, release, return. That repetition builds control faster than any correction ever could. Rainy day? Hide treats, make scent trails, roll kibble in towels. The goal isn't perfection—it's participation. The only wrong move is doing nothing.

Somewhere along the way, this stops being about training and becomes therapy. You rediscover patience. Your dog rediscovers trust. You stop seeing them as a problem and start seeing them as a partner who's been waiting for you to speak their language. Somewhere between the fiftieth recall and the hundredth muddy retrieve, the chaos becomes connection.

And for the love of all things chewed, stop calling it "exercise." It's fulfillment. It's how you turn destruction into devotion. You'll know you've hit it when they lie down afterward, exhale that deep satisfied sigh that says, *finally*. That isn't exhaustion—it's peace.

After two decades of working with these dogs, the pattern never changes. The happiest Labs all have structure. The broken ones—the ones filling shelters—never did. Humans ruin this breed with laziness and guilt. We buy them to feel active, then complain when they act alive. We confuse affection with purpose. Love doesn't fix boredom; work does.

Labs were engineered for purpose. You don't have to hunt or compete to honor that. You just have to give them a job.

Train, play, think, repeat. Every day. That's how you turn chaos into loyalty.

So when your Lab's pacing the living room, eyes wild, ball in mouth, tail clearing furniture—don't yell. That's not disobedience. That's a plea. It's your dog saying, *Give me something to do before I start my own project.*

Throw the ball. Hide the treat. Set the challenge. Channel the madness. Because a busy Lab doesn't destroy your home—it reminds you why you wanted one in the first place.

And that's the secret nobody tells you when you bring home your first Labrador: you don't tame the chaos. You work with it until it becomes joy.

Chapter 13
The Working Saint: How Labradors Save Us (Mostly from Ourselves)

Not every Labrador ends up shredding tennis balls in a suburban yard. Some of them get promoted. They graduate from chaos to purpose, from fetch to focus. The same instincts that make them hell on furniture also make them lifesavers, therapists, and emotional anchors. Give that energy a mission, and you get a dog that changes lives—sometimes literally.

Labs are the workhorses of the service world. They lead the blind, steady the unsteady, alert the diabetic, comfort the broken, and find the lost. And they do it with the same goofy grin they'd wear while stealing your sandwich. It's not magic. It's what happens when all that drive and sensitivity finally has somewhere meaningful to go.

The breed didn't get this reputation by accident. Labs have the holy trinity of service-dog traits: brains, brawn, and a bottomless desire to please (usually in exchange for snacks). They're strong enough to brace a human's weight, gentle enough to pick up a dropped credit card, and intuitive enough to sense a panic attack before it hits. That combination doesn't come from training alone—it's hardwired.

The Guiding Eyes of the World

Let's start with the classics: guide dogs for the visually impaired. If you've ever seen a Lab in a harness leading someone through a crowd, you've witnessed trust in its purest form. That dog isn't following commands; it's making decisions. It's judging traffic, curbs, noise, and chaos, then choosing the safest path forward. "Intelligent disobedience" is what they call it—disobeying a direct order if it would lead their person into danger. That takes guts and judgment most humans don't have on their best day.

Picture Luna, a young guide Lab leading her handler across a busy intersection. Horns blaring, people rushing, wind in her ears—and she stops cold at the curb when she sees a car rolling through a red light. Her person tells her "forward." She doesn't budge. The car zooms by. That's not obedience. That's partnership. That's what separates a pet from a professional.

Mobility and Assistance Work

Then you've got the Labs who give people back their independence. They open doors, pick up dropped keys, pull wheelchairs, and hit elevator buttons with noses so gentle it's almost surgical. It's not glamorous, but it's freedom. For someone who can't bend or balance, that single act means dignity.

I worked with a client named Sarah whose yellow Lab, Max, could fetch her phone from another room, bring her shoes one at a time, and alert her if the doorbell rang while she was asleep. Max wasn't just a helper—he was an extension of her body, a four-legged prosthetic made of loyalty and fur. Watching them work together was humbling. You could feel the silent rhythm between them: her voice, his action, their teamwork. Seamless.

The Nose That Saves Lives

Labs have noses that could embarrass a bloodhound. They can smell chemical changes in human bodies—tiny shifts in blood sugar, the subtle scent of a seizure before it hits. Diabetes alert dogs, seizure alert dogs, even dogs trained to detect allergens—all rely on that freakish olfactory genius.

Tom's Lab, Daisy, has been trained to alert when his blood sugar drops. She'll paw at his leg, then fetch a glucose kit from a specific drawer. She's beaten his continuous glucose monitor to the punch more than once. Science can measure a lot of things, but it still hasn't figured out how a dog can smell biochemistry and turn it into action faster than any machine.

The Emotional Frontline

Then there's the work no lab manual can teach: therapy and emotional support. These aren't task dogs—they're comfort incarnate. Hospitals, schools, disaster zones—Labs walk into the worst moments of human life and bring light with them. They don't need words; they just exist beside you until breathing feels easier again.

Bella, a chocolate Lab I met on a therapy rotation, spent her days lying beside kids in a children's hospital. No tricks, no fancy training—just patience and that soft, steady presence that says, You're safe. One kid told me, "She smells like home." That's it. That's the power. They give us back a piece of peace.

The Soldiers' Shadows

For veterans and trauma survivors, Labs become anchors. They're trained to recognize stress signals, interrupt panic spirals, and pull people back from the edge. When James, a combat veteran with PTSD, starts to hyperventilate, his Lab, Hunter, presses against him until the world quiets down. Hunter doesn't analyze or explain. He just stands there—a physical reminder that James isn't alone. The simplicity of it is what makes it sacred.

Heroes on the Hunt

And then there are the search-and-rescue dogs—the adrenaline junkies of the service world. Labs have been part of rescue teams for decades, combing through rubble after earthquakes, sniffing snowdrifts for avalanche victims, and finding missing hikers miles off trail. They work in disaster zones without complaint, tails wagging like they're on an adventure instead of a mission. Their reward? A toy and a pat. That's all they want.

I once watched a black Lab named Rocky work a collapsed building after a storm. Debris everywhere, twisted metal, noise, smoke—and that dog moved like a machine, nose down, tail up, pure focus. When he found a survivor, he barked once, sharp and certain. That bark cut through chaos like hope itself.

School Dogs and Reading Buddies

Labs even go to school—literally. Reading programs across the country use calm, gentle dogs to help kids practice reading aloud without fear of judgment. A kid who won't say a word to a teacher will read a whole story to a dog that listens like it's Shakespeare. It's quiet magic, the kind humans keep trying to replicate in apps and fail miserably at.

Crisis Response and Comfort Teams

After tragedies—natural disasters, mass trauma, loss—Labs show up again. Not with answers, but with presence. A golden-eyed shadow that sits beside grief and makes it bearable. Their calm energy spreads like gravity; people just breathe easier around them. You can't fake that. You can only be that.

Lucy, a yellow Lab brought in after a school shooting, sat for hours while people cried into her fur. She didn't move, didn't flinch, just absorbed the storm until they could stand again. That's not something you train. That's grace in a dog suit.

Why Labradors? Because they feel everything. They're emotional sponges with no filter. Your joy, your fear, your pain—they take it all in, process it, and hand it back in a calmer form. That's what makes them such brilliant working dogs and such terrible poker players. You always know exactly what a Lab's thinking, and that's precisely why humans trust them with their lives.

The truth is, not every Lab is cut out for service work. It takes the right temperament: steady, confident, unflappable. The ones who make it through training aren't just obedient—they're professionals. And when they retire, they don't stop giving. They just move into family life like they've been waiting for it all along.

You could fill pages with the lives Labs have changed, the people they've saved, the comfort they've given—but it all comes down to one truth: these dogs remind us what we were supposed to be. Loyal. Steady. Kind. They don't ask for much in return—just a job and a place to belong.

That's the Labrador's secret. They don't chase glory. They don't need applause. They just keep showing up, tail wagging, heart open, doing the work nobody else wants to do.

And if that's not sainthood, I don't know what is.

CHAPTER 14
THE FAMILY CIRCUS: LABRADORS, CHILDREN, AND OTHER UNSUPERVISED MAMMALS

Families always tell me, "We wanted a Lab because they're great with kids." And I always smile the kind of smile people give before walking into traffic. Yes, Labs *can* be amazing with children—loyal, gentle, patient. But let's be honest: they're also hyper, impulsive, and built like living bowling balls. That "perfect family dog" fantasy usually lasts until the toddler gets body-checked into a wall during a game of fetch.

Labs and kids have a lot in common. Both are loud, sticky, and convinced gravity doesn't apply to them. Both think rules are optional and both crash hard after ten minutes of chaos. The difference is, one of them has teeth that can crack a femur and the other cries when you say "no." Put them together unsupervised and you're basically running an experiment in physics and poor judgment.

Here's the rule nobody wants to say out loud: your Lab isn't a babysitter. They're another child that happens to have better hearing and worse impulse control. Treat them like family, yes—but family with boundaries, supervision, and a zero-trust policy until proven otherwise.

The first mistake people make is thinking the dog "understands." No, they don't. They tolerate. Big difference. That slobbery smile when your toddler hugs them? Half affection, half survival instinct. Labs are famously patient, but patience isn't infinite. Every nip, growl, or side-eye starts with ignored signals. If a dog's lip curls, tail stiffens, or they turn their head away, that's not "cute." That's the warning label you didn't read.

Introduce babies and dogs like you're handling live explosives. Controlled distance, calm energy, short exposures. Let the dog sniff from afar, reward calm, never force contact. Don't plop the baby on the dog "for the photo." I don't care how many likes you think it'll get. You're teaching your dog that small humans are unpredictable and inescapable, which is the fast track to resentment.

As the kid grows, you train *both species*. The Lab learns impulse control around flailing limbs. The kid learns that tails are not handles. "Gentle" means gentle, not "grab and squeal." Toddlers need leash training almost as much as the dog does. I tell parents: never trust a silence that involves both child and Lab. One of them is plotting, and it's never good.

Playtime is where things go from sweet to stupid in seconds. You start with fetch. The kid throws the ball. The dog chases. Everyone laughs. Then the dog forgets the ball and goes for the kid's sleeve. Suddenly we've got tears and a lecture about "aggression." No, that's not aggression— that's overstimulation. You wound the dog up, then forgot to bring them back down. Play in short bursts, end before chaos hits, and never mix high-energy games with tiny humans who can't read dog body language.

Labs don't know their own strength. They crash into kids because they're thrilled, not malicious. But tell that to a five-year-old who just got flattened. This is why "down" and "leave it" aren't optional tricks—they're survival tools. If your Lab doesn't have those two commands solid, your furniture and your family are on borrowed time.

And then there's food. Kids drop it, Labs inhale it, and everyone screams. Food guarding starts with chaos. Control the environment. The Lab eats behind a gate. Kids don't approach during meals. Period. Don't make your dog defend what's theirs because you thought it'd be "cute" to hand-feed. Respect prevents problems better than correction ever will.

Speaking of correction—stop punishing normal dog reactions. If your Lab growls when a kid grabs its ear, that's communication. It's not betrayal, it's a warning. Punishing the growl teaches them to skip the warning next time. Congratulations, you just created a dog that bites "out of nowhere."

Every family has *that* relative—the Grandma who ignores every rule. "Oh, he just loves me, I can sneak him food!" or "Don't be silly, he'd never hurt anyone." Those people are chaos accelerators. You need to manage them, too. Post rules on the fridge if you have to: no rough play, no hand-feeding, no unsupervised time. Family gatherings bring stress, noise, and food everywhere. That's a sensory-overload buffet for a Lab. Create quiet zones. Give the dog a retreat space before they snap.

Let's talk overstimulation. It's not just the zoomies; it's full sensory meltdown. Too many people, too much noise, too many smells—your dog hits redline. They pant, pace, grab toys, start mouthing or jumping, and you think they're "being bad." They're trying to regulate. Step in early. Leash up, guide them away, calm them down. It's the equivalent of putting a kid in time-out before they explode.

And for the love of decency, stop assuming a wagging tail means happiness. It means arousal—could be excitement, could be anxiety. A wag doesn't mean "I'm fine." It means "I'm charged." Read the rest of the body. Is the dog loose and wiggly, or stiff and silent? You don't need a degree in behavior; you just need to pay attention.

Every Lab owner with kids eventually learns this the hard way. I once worked with a family whose six-year-old kept "playing horsey" on their two-year-old Lab. They thought it was adorable. The dog tolerated it—until one day it didn't. A nip, a scream, a frantic call to me. They were lucky it was a warning bite. That dog wasn't dangerous. The humans were reckless. We retrained the *people*. The Lab got decompression walks, structure, and peace. The kid got boundaries. Everyone lived.

Then comes the adolescent phase—the teenage dog meets toddler problem. The calm puppy everyone bragged about turns into a hormonal linebacker overnight. Suddenly he's jumping again, stealing toys, and pretending "sit" is optional. Parents think the dog forgot his manners. Nope—his brain short-circuited. Keep supervision airtight, double down on structure, and remind the kids the rules didn't disappear because the dog grew taller. The teenage Lab is physically grown but mentally feral. Treat him like a loaded spring until he grows his brain back.

Bite inhibition is another one of those misunderstood topics. Labs are mouthy; it's in their DNA. They explore with teeth.

The goal isn't "never bite." It's "bite softly." Puppies learn that from littermates; adult dogs learn it from consistent correction. Yelp once, redirect to a toy, praise the calm. Don't slap, don't scream, and don't confuse the dog by laughing when it happens "playfully." You're not teaching "no bite"—you're teaching "control yourself."

And yes, Labs can coexist beautifully with children. I've seen them nap beside babies, shadow toddlers, and herd preteens away from driveways like tiny security guards. But it works because the adults put in the work—supervision, training, management, consistency. You don't earn that harmony through good vibes. You earn it through repetition and boundaries.

Here's the ugly truth most families ignore: 90 percent of "dog bites" in homes could have been prevented by adult supervision. You can't delegate safety to instinct. Even the best Lab has limits. The dog's job isn't to tolerate endless poking; your job is to intervene before it happens. That's not paranoia—it's responsibility.

And when something *does* go wrong, everyone blames the dog. It's easier than admitting we dropped the ball. But guilt doesn't fix behavior—leadership does. You can't correct what you won't own. Stop pointing at the fur-covered scapegoat and start managing the environment that failed both of you.

Now toss another dog into the mix and the chaos goes exponential. Two Labs together are an improv troupe with no stage manager. Rough play turns into collisions, kids scream, energy spikes, and suddenly you're refereeing a fur tornado. Manage introductions, split feeding, rotate playtime, and never assume "they'll work it out." Friendly doesn't mean friction-free. Dogs can love each other and still need boundaries.

Every now and then, I meet a family that gets it right. They set rules early. They teach their kids to read signals. They give the dog a crate that's off-limits. They keep play gentle and structured. The result? A home where respect runs both ways. The dog doesn't just behave—they thrive. You can see it in the way they move: confident, calm, comfortable in the chaos because someone finally gave them a framework.

And the kids learn, too. They grow up understanding empathy, respect, and how to handle boundaries—lessons half of adulthood still struggles with. That's the magic of raising dogs and children together *correctly*. It teaches everyone that love without rules isn't love—it's selfishness wrapped in sentimentality.

So, if you're reading this while your Lab drags a child across the yard by a sleeve, stop romanticizing the chaos. Manage it. Structure it. Teach both sides how to coexist. The dog's not the problem. The lack of management is.

Your Lab doesn't need to be a nanny, a babysitter, or a therapy dog. They just need to be safe, understood, and supervised. They'll give back tenfold—loyalty, laughter, the kind of unconditional affection that'll ruin you for normal relationships. But they need your leadership to get there.

Because at the end of the day, the equation is simple: one overstimulated Lab + one unpredictable kid = one preventable disaster. Your job is to stop it before it happens.

The families who nail this don't end up with perfect dogs. They end up with trust. Kids who grow up respecting living things. Dogs who relax because someone finally sees them. That's the payoff for all the rules: peace without fear, chaos without danger.

So set the rules. Hold the line. And when the house is full of noise and fur and laughter, remember: this is what family looks like when everyone's finally doing their damn job.

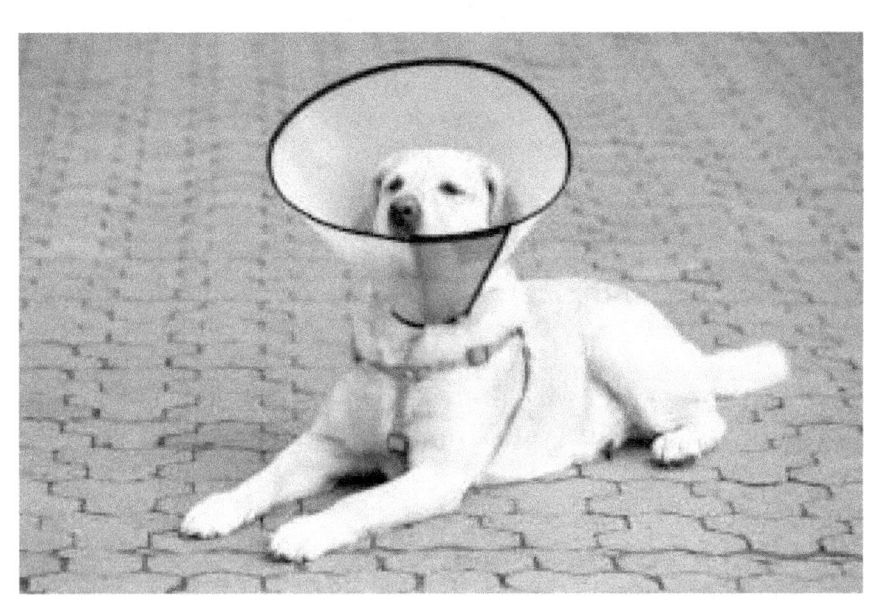

CHAPTER 15
THE SOCIAL BUTTERFLY: WHY "FRIENDLY" ISN'T ALWAYS A COMPLIMENT

People love to say, "Labs are so social!" as if that's always a compliment. What they mean is, "My dog has no personal space awareness and greets strangers like a frat boy at spring break." Social? Sure. Polite? Not even close.

The Labrador is the golden retriever's loud cousin who drinks too much at the party, hugs everyone, and knocks over the charcuterie board before passing out in the punch bowl. That's the "friendly" everyone brags about. Somewhere along the way, we decided chaos equals confidence and started calling it sociability.

Here's the truth: Labs are born extroverts with zero filter. That's fun until you've got 80 pounds of affection slamming into your guests' knees while you're yelling, "He's friendly!" across the living room. Spoiler: no one cares that he's friendly when their wine is now part of your carpet.

Politeness isn't optional—it's survival. Because in the real world, "friendly" dogs get kicked, banned, or worse when they overwhelm the wrong person.

The first thing to fix? Door greetings. I've seen entire families taken out by a single Labrador with a tail like a Louisville Slugger. Guests ring the bell, the dog explodes like someone lit dynamite under his ribs, and the next thirty seconds are a blur of barking, jumping, and joy-vomit. Everyone acts surprised, as if this doesn't happen every damn time.

Teach the dog to wait. Leash them before opening the door. Make sitting the price of attention. It's not about dominance—it's physics management. You're trying to prevent concussions. If your guests can't enter without signing a waiver, your Lab isn't "excited," they're untrained.

And let's talk about jumping. Labs jump because people reward it. You squeal, you pet, you laugh—it's basically applause. Dogs don't understand "get down" when your hands are still on them. Turn your back, fold your arms, stand still. Reward the sit, ignore the chaos. Consistency beats drama every time.

Now, add food to the mix and you've got a hostage situation. A Labrador's moral compass collapses around appetizers. They'll counter-surf, dumpster-dive, and inhale anything left within snout range. I once watched a Lab swallow a full rotisserie chicken bones and all before his owner could blink. Three grand in emergency vet bills later, he survived, and they still said, "He's just food-motivated." No—he's unsupervised.

Here's a fun rule of thumb: if it smells edible, your Lab has already made a plan to steal it. You can fix this with boundaries. Teach "leave it" like your life depends on it. Keep trash locked, food out of reach, and relatives informed. Because nothing ruins Thanksgiving faster than explaining to Grandma that her stuffing is now "bioavailable."

The "friendly with everyone" myth extends to dogs, too, and that's where people really lose the plot. Labs love to meet others—but not all other dogs love to meet them. Your dog's enthusiasm can look like harassment to a nervous or reactive dog. The phrase "he just wants to play" has preceded more fights than I can count. Translation: "I don't control my dog and I'm hoping yours is patient."

Leash manners aren't decoration—they're diplomacy. A well-trained Lab should heel calmly past other dogs, not drag you into traffic in the name of friendship. You wouldn't let your kid run across a restaurant to hug strangers, right? Same idea.

Now we get to the battlefield of bad decisions: the dog park. Every Lab owner thinks their dog will thrive there, because "he's so social." I've spent decades breaking up park brawls started by "social" dogs who don't understand boundaries. Dog parks are like unsupervised recess for toddlers with knives.

Your dog doesn't learn good behavior there—they learn mob psychology. The confident get louder, the insecure get bullied, and the humans stand around scrolling their phones. Half of those "play" sessions are dominance rehearsals or resource-guarding matches waiting to detonate.

If you insist on going, treat it like a minefield. Pick low-traffic hours. Keep moving so your dog follows *you*, not the mob. Interrupt play every few minutes for recalls and calm breaks. If tails stiffen, hackles rise, or one dog starts humping like it's a job interview—leash up and leave. It's not worth the vet bill or the lawsuit.

And about those lawsuits: people underestimate how fast "friendly" can turn into "liability." All it takes is one startled jogger, one jump that knocks over a kid, or one small dog pinned during rough play. The other owner doesn't care that your Lab meant well. The law doesn't either. "He's never done that before" is not a legal defense.

If you really want socialization, ditch the park and do structured playdates with known, balanced dogs. Two or three good friends are better than fifty strangers who might hate each other. Think of it like human friendships—quality over quantity. Your Lab doesn't need to love everyone; they need to behave around everyone.

Multi-dog households are their own circus. Labs tend to become the loudest voice in the pack, not the leader. They're enthusiasm incarnate—always the first to start play, the last to quit, and the most likely to trigger chaos. Balance comes from structure: separate feeding, supervised play, enforced downtime. Don't let them practice mayhem together. It's cute until it's property damage.

In homes with smaller dogs or cats, introduce slowly. The Lab's chase instinct can kick in fast. Keep leashes on, reward calm, never let rough play escalate. The moment you hear yelps or see paws on a smaller animal's back, game over. Interrupt, redirect, decompress. You're not a buzzkill—you're the adult in the room.

Then there are guests who bring dogs. That's where friendships die. Never assume visiting dogs and resident dogs will "work it out." They won't. Neutral ground introductions, parallel walks, separate toys, and crate time save lives. Don't wait for tension—you'll see it in the stiff posture and hard stare long before the growl. Intervene early or you'll be calling me at midnight asking how to break up a fight without losing fingers.

Leash reactivity is another misunderstood gem. Everyone thinks "reactive" means aggressive. It doesn't. Labs pull, bark, or lunge out of frustration, excitement, or pure FOMO. They want to meet the world and the leash gets in the way. That frustration builds until it looks like rage. The fix? Teach calm before exposure. Distance, focus, repetition. You can't fix arousal with more arousal.

And if your Lab's the kind who turns into a pogo stick every time someone walks by, congratulations—you own the most common Labrador problem on Earth. Over-arousal is baked into their wiring. You manage it, not cure it. Mental work before social outings, leashed decompression walks after, and a calm human at the other end of the leash. Your mood drives theirs; if you're tense, they're chaos.

Let's be real—most public Labrador embarrassments start with owner optimism. You say "He's good!" right before he body-slams a stroller. You tell the trainer "He's usually fine" right before he face-plants in a mud puddle. Humility saves lives. Assume he's one distraction away from disaster and you'll actually prepare.

There's also a dark side to the "therapy dog" myth. Everyone wants to believe their Lab is destined for hospital visits and emotional-support stardom. Some are. Most aren't. Therapy work requires bombproof stability, not just sweetness. If your dog startles at loud noises, jumps on strangers, or panics when separated, they're not ready. Forcing them into that role doesn't make you compassionate—it makes you reckless. Let your dog be what they are. Not every Labrador wants to fix humanity. Some just want to chase tennis balls and nap in air-conditioning.

And yes, your Lab can embarrass you in ways you didn't know were possible. I've seen one rip open a stranger's backpack for granola bars, another knock over a priest, and one who stole an entire baguette off a café table mid-stride. Every single owner said the same thing: "He's never done that before." Sure. Until he did. Because he's a Labrador—curiosity, hunger, and chaos fused into a meat missile.

Good manners aren't about obedience trophies—they're about self-defense. A polite Lab keeps their reputation, and yours, intact. You never want to be "that owner." The one everyone avoids at the park, the one whose dog "plays too rough," the one who's always apologizing through nervous laughter.

Speaking of apologies: if you need to say sorry for your dog, mean it. Don't follow it with excuses or jokes. Own the moment. "I'm sorry he jumped, I'm working on it." Period. Then walk away and fix it. People forgive sincerity. They don't forgive denial.

Being in public with a Labrador is like walking around with a celebrity toddler. Everyone wants to interact, and your job is crowd control. Strangers will reach out without asking, kids will squeal, and old ladies will try to feed them cookies. Your Lab will love it, but that's not the point. You protect your dog from their own enthusiasm by saying "No, not today." Boundaries aren't cruelty; they're clarity.

Here's the quiet truth no one tells new owners: your dog's manners are your reflection. Every sloppy greeting, every leash-dragging disaster, every park fight traced back to "he's friendly" damages more than your ego—it erodes the public's trust in dogs like him. Good behavior protects all of them.

So put in the work. Practice calm greetings until they're boring. Teach "wait" at doorways like it's gospel. Walk in public like you own the sidewalk but respect the space. Reward neutrality, not just excitement.

When it all clicks, it's magic. You'll see your Lab navigate a crowd with grace, ignore the barking dog across the street, sit politely while a kid pets them. That's not luck—that's leadership. And for the first time, people won't say "he's friendly." They'll say "he's well-trained."

That's the goal. Not perfection. Not sainthood. Just a Labrador who can exist in public without turning it into a spectacle. A dog who represents every good thing about the breed instead of every bad stereotype.

Because at the end of the day, manners are armor. They keep your dog safe, your reputation intact, and the breed's legacy alive.

So when you clip on that leash, remember—you're not walking a Labrador. You're walking a billboard that says, "This is what responsibility looks like." Make it worth reading.

CHAPTER 16
TRAVEL, ADVENTURES, AND OTHER BAD IDEAS WITH A LABRADOR

There's a fantasy every Lab owner has at least once: the perfect day outdoors. The sun's shining, your dog's off-leash, you're tossing a ball across a sparkling lake while people smile admiringly at your "well-trained companion." Then reality shows up: your dog cannonballs into a swamp, eats half a goose turd, rolls in something dead, and vanishes into the woods like a furry convict on the run.

That's not failure. That's a Labrador.

These dogs were built for adventure—literally engineered for cold water, rough terrain, and bad decisions. Which is why every outing is a balancing act between joy and regret. They live for it, and if you're smart, you'll learn to love it too. But only after you accept one rule: freedom is earned, not assumed.

Let's start with travel.

Everyone swears their Lab "loves car rides." What they mean is their dog loses its mind at the sound of keys. Most Labs treat the back seat like a rave in a washing machine. There's drool on the windows, nose prints on the mirrors, hair embedded in the upholstery like biological glitter. And that smell? That's what hope smells like after it's been marinated in dog breath and lake water.

Crates or crash-tested harnesses aren't optional—they're non-negotiable. You're not being "mean" for crating them in the car; you're being responsible. That sixty-pound missile of love becomes a lethal projectile in a fender bender. I've seen Labs crash through dashboards because someone said,

"He likes to look out the window." So does chaos. Buckle it in.

And for the record, if your Lab pants and cries in the car, that's not excitement—it's overstimulation. You're basically revving a Ferrari in traffic. Calm starts before ignition. Short rides, soft praise, no baby talk. You're conditioning focus, not karaoke.

Then there's the packing list. Every trip turns you into a sherpa. Towels. Water. First-aid kit. Leashes. Long lines. Poop bags. Snacks. Spare snacks. Extra towels for the towels. A tarp for your trunk because that "quick dip" is about to cost you an interior detail. Forget one thing, and your Lab will exploit it. No leash? Perfect, time to chase ducks. No towel? Great, now your car's a biology experiment.

You finally get there—trailhead, beach, lake, whatever—and your Lab bursts out like they're auditioning for a National Geographic special. This is the moment you realize "adventure dog" is a full-time job.

Trail etiquette matters. Keep them leashed until you're absolutely sure they can recall off distraction. "He always comes when I call" doesn't count when there's a squirrel involved. Off-leash isn't a vibe; it's a privilege. If your dog barrels up to strangers, you're not friendly—you're rude. "He just wants to say hi" has caused more fights, injuries, and angry hikers than actual aggression ever has.

Here's how recall actually works: you build it like religion. It's not a word; it's a promise. You start small, reinforce heavily, and never—ever—use their name in anger. If you've screamed "Bailey, get over here!" while shaking a leash like a maniac, congratulations—you've turned your recall cue into white noise. Use long lines, high-value rewards, and timing like your sanity depends on it. Because it does.

Freedom feels good right up until it doesn't. The number of "he's never run off before" stories that end in tears could fill a library. I've found Labs miles from campsites, covered in ticks, smiling like it was worth it. They always come back—eventually—but the road between "eventually" and "immediately" is paved with panic.

And then there's water. The Lab's natural habitat. Lakes, rivers, puddles, your toilet—they see liquid and instinct takes over. Swimming is their birthright, but that doesn't mean it's safe. Cold shock, undertow, exhaustion—it's all real. Keep swim sessions short, throw from safe ground, and don't let them drink half the lake. Giardia isn't a fun souvenir.

And when they're done? That's when the real suffering begins. The post-swim shake. You'll know it's coming because they look at you first. It's personal. Every Lab has a sixth sense for the exact moment when maximum splash radius can be achieved. Congratulations—you're now wearing Eau de Wet Dog.

That smell doesn't leave. Ever. It soaks into your soul. You can scrub, towel, or pray, but the scent will cling until you question your life choices. And that's before they roll in dirt to "dry off." I've had Labs turn beige to black in 30 seconds flat, grinning like they cured sadness.

Adventure with a Lab is a cycle of joy, chaos, regret, cleanup, and memory. The cleanup part is the longest. You'll hose them down, dry them off, and watch in despair as they shake again in the living room. Then you'll vacuum. Then they'll shake again. This is your life now.

Trail manners extend beyond dogs. Labs are people dogs, which means they'll greet every stranger like a long-lost friend. Teach "leave it" and "watch me" early. Not everyone likes being body-slammed by affection. Some hikers carry trekking poles for balance, not jousting. Respect other people's space.

And wildlife? Oh, they'll find it. Squirrels, rabbits, birds, fish, trash—Labs think everything's a team sport. A strong recall and leash control keep you from starring in your own viral video titled "Local Idiot Chases Dog Through National Park." Don't let your dog learn the hard way that porcupines bite back.

Camping with Labs is another level of comedy. You've got the gear, the tent, the fire—and the dog who thinks it's all edible. Labs love firewood, sleeping bags, and anything that crinkles. They'll step on your face at 3 a.m., bark at ghosts, and fart in a confined space like they're testing your marriage. Bring wipes, patience, and a sense of humor.

And that friend—the one with the "perfect off-leash Lab"? They're lying. Every single one of them has a story they're not telling. The day their dog chased a deer. The time he disappeared for an hour. The emergency vet visit for "mystery stomach contents." They'll smile and say, "Oh, he never runs off." Sure. Until he does.

Freedom isn't magic; it's math. You earn it with consistency, recall drills, proofing distractions, and building trust one outing at a time. The dog who listens off-leash in the forest is the product of hundreds of boring backyard reps you didn't post on Instagram.

When the hike's over and your Lab finally collapses in the back seat, you'll think, *that was worth it.* And it is. Because watching a Lab run full tilt through open space is like seeing pure joy wearing a fur coat. It's the reason we put up with the mess. But the work doesn't end there.

Post-adventure care is a ritual. Check ears, paws, and eyes for debris. Rinse their coat. Dry thoroughly—moisture trapped under that double coat is an invitation to yeast infections. Brush out burrs and mats before they turn into vet bills. And for the love of sanity, clean the car before the smell evolves into something sentient.

Labs are prone to ear infections because their ears trap moisture like Tupperware. After every swim, dry them out with a soft towel or an ear solution. Don't wait for the head-shaking symphony that ends with a vet visit and antibiotics.

Hydration matters too. A tired Lab will drink anything—puddles, lakes, ditches. Carry clean water and collapsible bowls. Dehydration hides behind excitement. You think they're fine until they crash hard later.

Adventure Labs burn calories like engines. Bring real fuel. High-protein snacks, not gas-station junk. The goal is to end the trip tired, not broken. You want a satisfied dog, not a wreck.

And while we're on exhaustion—Labs don't self-regulate. They'll swim until they sink. They'll chase until their pads bleed. They'll run on fumes just to make you happy. You have to be the one with the sense to call it. When they start slowing down, drooling excessively, or tripping on terrain, it's time to rest. Their heart will keep saying "yes" long after their body says "stop."

You'll learn to pack like a professional. A checklist isn't optional—it's survival. Leash, harness, first aid, life jacket, towels, brush, waste bags, ID tags, snacks, water, booties if terrain's rough. Every item's there because one day you'll forget it and pay the price.

Here's a free lesson: always bring two leashes. You'll drop one in the river. Always pack more towels than you think you need. You don't. And never, ever forget the treats. Training doesn't stop just because the scenery changed.

If this sounds like a lot of work, that's because it is. But this is what the breed was built for—movement, partnership, purpose. The Labrador isn't complete sitting on a couch. They need open air, new smells, and a task to chew on that isn't your shoe.

The best part? Watching it click. That moment when your recall lands perfectly. When your Lab checks in mid-adventure without being called. When they swim back and drop the toy at your feet instead of vanishing downstream. That's the reward. Not the Instagram photo, not the compliments—just that shared moment of "we get each other now."

And sometimes, despite all the prep, they'll still screw up. They'll roll in goose crap five minutes before the car. They'll shake mud into your coffee. They'll find the one patch of poison oak in the county. You'll sigh, curse, and laugh, because deep down, you know this is exactly who they are.

Adventure with a Lab isn't about control—it's about coexistence. You'll never beat their instincts. You just learn to channel them into something that doesn't end in property damage. Freedom is a contract between chaos and training. Break your end, and you'll spend the weekend chasing a blur of joy through the woods. Keep your end, and you'll have a partner who'd follow you into the ocean and back.

By the time you're home, the dog's asleep before the engine's off. You'll carry them inside, towel them one last time, and swear you're never doing this again. Then, a week later, you'll pack the car anyway. Because you'll miss it—the smell, the mud, the ridiculous happiness.

That's the thing about Labs. They ruin your car, wreck your plans, and steal your heart, usually in that order. But they remind you what freedom actually means. Not chaos for chaos's sake—but the kind you earn through trust, repetition, and shared experience.

Adventure with a Labrador isn't a vacation. It's a test. But pass it, and you'll never want to travel without them again.

Chapter 17
Gray Muzzles and Gold Hearts: Returning the Favor

One day you'll wake up and your Labrador won't be waiting at the door like a caffeinated intern. They'll still wag, but slower. They'll stretch before standing, then glance at you like, "Hang on, give me a second." And that's when it hits you: the unstoppable force that used to launch itself through life is getting old.

No one tells you when it happens. There's no calendar reminder for "the first time he can't jump in the truck." You just notice it in flashes—the hesitation at the stairs, the softer bark, the way he watches you walk away instead of following. At first you tell yourself it's nothing. "He's just tired." Then you realize he's tired more often. Denial is the first stage of dog aging, and it's brutal.

Labs don't fade quietly. They go down fighting—still trying to chase balls they can't catch, still insisting they're fine as they limp back to you with pride in every stiff step. That's what makes it hard. You have to protect them from themselves.

Those long runs and marathon swims? They become slow walks and wading. And it's on you to make that adjustment, because they won't. They'll keep going until they break something trying to make you happy. So you trade distance for dignity. Ten minutes of sniffing beats two hours of pain. The new adventure is slower, smaller, but no less sacred.

The body tells the story first. The hips go. The stairs become mountains. The floor gets slippery. You start throwing rugs down like a paranoid grandma. Ramps become part of your décor. You lift them into the car and pretend your back doesn't hurt because you can't stand the look they give you when they realize they needed help.

Joint care isn't optional—it's triage. Glucosamine, fish oil, anti-inflammatories, pain meds, acupuncture, laser therapy—whatever buys comfort, do it. Don't cheap out. You spent years laughing at their chaos; now you pay it back with care. Pain isn't "just old age." It's pain. And ignoring it doesn't make you stoic; it makes you negligent.

Then there's the brain. That's the one that guts you. The confusion, the nighttime pacing, the moments they stare at a wall or forget why they came into a room. Canine cognitive decline is real. It sneaks in quietly, like a fog. You'll see them stand in the yard, unsure which door leads home. You'll call their name and watch them search your face for a second longer than before.

This is where patience replaces pride. You guide them through the fog like a friend, not a boss. Keep routines simple. Don't move furniture. Keep nights calm, lights soft. Talk to them even when they look past you—they can still hear the love in your voice. And when they forget, remind them. Every damn day.

Old Labs still need purpose. Maybe it's carrying a toy from one room to another. Maybe it's supervising laundry. Give them jobs that make them feel useful. A bored senior is a depressed one. They don't know retirement; they only know rhythm. Keep that rhythm going, even if it's slower, even if it's mostly naps and gentle walks.

Diet shifts, too. Senior dogs burn fewer calories but still need protein for muscle. Go for quality, not hype. Skip fad diets and boutique "miracle foods." Keep weight down; extra pounds are extra pain. And keep water nearby—dehydration sneaks up faster when they move less.

Vet visits become your new normal. Not just for shots, but for monitoring kidneys, liver, thyroid, joints. Find a vet who treats you like a partner, not a wallet. Senior care is detective work—small signs mean everything. Don't wait for collapse. A month can make the difference between management and regret.

You'll get used to the sound of your own worry. Every limp, every sigh, every skipped meal feels like the start of the end.

That's the mental toll nobody warns you about. The emotional math of aging dogs is cruel: you know how this story ends, and you live it anyway.

Some days they'll rally. Out of nowhere, they'll bound like they're three again. You'll cry, smile, and then realize you're crying *because* you smiled. Those moments are gifts—tiny miracles in fur coats. Don't ruin them by counting how many you have left. Just take them.

And then there's the other part. The part everyone avoids talking about until they can't avoid it anymore: the long goodbye.

Labs don't know what "goodbye" means, but they understand love better than any language we've invented. They'll keep showing up for you until they can't. You'll see it in their eyes first—the quiet plea for help you hoped you'd never have to answer. The walk that used to take twenty minutes now takes forty. They start to fall behind, not from stubbornness, but because the engine's running out of gas.

You'll lie to yourself. "He still eats. He still wags." You'll list reasons to wait. You'll make deals with the universe, like you did when they were sick as puppies. But deep down, you'll know. Every good owner knows. Love becomes the willingness to stop the suffering you can't fix.

And that's the hardest, kindest thing you'll ever do.

You'll hold them, talk to them, and feel the weight leave their body. You'll hate yourself for the relief. You'll go home to silence so heavy it vibrates. The bowls will still be there. The hair will still cling to everything. The house will feel too clean.

But here's the thing about dogs, especially Labs: they never really leave. You'll still step over imaginary tails. You'll still look for them when something drops in the kitchen. You'll still swear you hear the collar jingle in another room. Memory fills the space where muscle used to be.

I've buried more dogs than I want to count. The first few broke me. I kept thinking if I'd done more, fed better, walked longer, I could've delayed it. Then I realized that wasn't the point. They weren't supposed to last forever. They were supposed to make you better while they were here. And they did. Every single time.

They teach you patience when they're young, humility when they're grown, and grace when they're old. That's the deal we sign without reading the fine print. They'll burn bright, fast, and leave us better than they found us.

If you're in the senior years right now—if your Lab's muzzle is more snow than coal, if their steps are slower, if their naps last longer—don't drown in dread. Focus on comfort. Quality over quantity. Warm beds, soft voices, short walks, long naps. They don't want pity; they want peace.

You'll find small joys again. The slow wag. The deep sigh when they settle beside you. The way they still look at you like you hung the moon. You'll start to love the quiet moments more than the wild ones. Because you know now what they cost.

Make home easier. Rugs for traction. Ramps for stairs. Orthopedic beds. Keep them warm; old bones hate cold floors. Massage their hips. Brush them gently. Talk to them like you always did. They don't need grand gestures—just presence.

And don't underestimate the emotional side for you. Watching them fade hurts like hell. There's guilt, frustration, grief before the grief. Some days you'll resent the responsibility, then hate yourself for feeling that way. That's normal. You're not weak for being tired. You're human for staying.

When the end does come, you'll want to hide from it. You'll tell yourself you can't watch. But if you can, stay. They spent their life trusting you to show up. Don't make the last thing they see a stranger. Let it be you—their person, the one constant from chaos to calm. Hold their head, whisper their name, thank them.

And afterward, don't rush to "move on." Sit with it. Grieve loud, grieve ugly. Every great dog deserves a human wrecked in their honor. That's grief doing its job, reminding you what mattered. Then, when the ache turns into memory instead of panic, you'll know they did their job.

Because that's the unspoken truth of the senior years—they prepare you. Slowly, gently, they teach you how to let go while still holding on. Every gray hair, every soft exhale, every slow walk is a rehearsal for goodbye.

You'll never be ready. You'll do it anyway.

And somewhere down the line, you'll see another Lab. Same goofy smile, same spark in the eyes, and your heart will flinch. You'll swear you're not ready for another. Then one day you'll realize the best way to honor the one you lost is to give another a shot at the same love. Not to replace— but to continue.

The chaos comes back. The fur returns. The circle starts again.

But it's different now. You move slower. You notice more. You laugh at the same messes that used to frustrate you. Because you've seen how fast it all goes. You know what those wild, young years are leading to, and you cherish them even harder.

That's what the gray muzzles teach us—that time's not the enemy, it's the gift. They gave you their best years. The least you can do is make their last ones gentle.

So ease their pain. Adjust your schedule. Carry them when you have to.
Sit in the grass with them one more time.
Tell them they did good.
And when it's over, remember every version of them... the puppy, the maniac, the guardian, the old soul who
watched over you long after they could keep up.

The Labrador doesn't fear aging. They just keep loving until their body quits. The rest is our lesson to learn: love hard, let go gently, and never take the good years for granted.

Because someday you'll miss the sound of their nails on the floor, the smell of wet fur, even the mess. And when that happens, you'll know—you did it right.

You gave them everything they needed: work, purpose, laughter, and a soft landing.

And in return, they gave you everything that mattered.

Chapter 18
Second Chances: Rescue, Redemption, and the Dogs Who Dare You to Earn It

Not every Labrador starts life in a nursery full of ribbons and promises. Some come from backyards, parking lots, or worse. People love to say *rescued* like it's a badge of honor. It's not. It's a story, and it usually begins where someone else gave up.

You see it in their eyes the first day. They look at you but not *into* you—like they're measuring the exits. You reach for the leash and they freeze. You toss a toy and they flinch. You tell your friends, "He's shy." Translation: someone broke him. You don't need to know how; he already does. What matters now is what you do next.

Shelters call it the honeymoon period. I call it the danger zone. The first thirty days decide whether that dog stays or goes back. Half of returned Labs come in during that window because people expected instant gratitude instead of slow trust. I've seen it happen too many times: adopter shows up, eyes shining, promising forever. Two weeks later, they're crying in the parking lot saying, "He just won't love us back." The dog doesn't understand; he just knows the car ride feels familiar again. That moment destroys something in him—the belief that home can last.

If you're reading this before you adopt, good. Know that forever takes time. A month isn't bonding; it's orientation. Don't expect fireworks. Expect confusion, silence, pacing, sleepless nights. That's what healing looks like in the beginning. Everyone screws this part up. They throw welcome-home parties, post photos, invite the neighbors. Congratulations, you just dropped a shell-shocked creature into a carnival. What they need is calm—no guests, no chaos, no expectations. Feed, walk, rest. Repeat. You're not bonding yet; you're proving predictability. That's the first real act of love.

Once they realize you're not sending them back, the mask cracks. Barking, guarding, panic when you leave. This is where people start Googling "rehome options." Don't. You're finally meeting the real dog. Trust isn't built through perfection; it's built through survival. Routine saves both of you. Same walk, same meal times, same rules. Predictability is safety. It's boring, but boring heals faster than pity ever will.

Some Labs come with more stamps in their paperwork than your passport. Two homes, three, maybe more. Each one left a mark. They've learned that humans are temporary and promises expire. Those dogs don't give trust—you earn it with quiet days and fair reactions. When one of them finally drops their guard, it feels like winning the lottery you didn't buy a ticket for.

You'll never know what sets them off until it happens. Men in hats. Brooms. Loud doors. The smell of beer. Triggers are ghosts from their past. Don't punish fear. Don't baby it either. Stand steady. Say, "You're safe," and mean it. Over time the ghosts get quieter.

Let's kill the savior myth while we're here. If you adopt because you want to feel noble, you're already screwing up. Rescue isn't about you. It's about the dog learning life doesn't suck anymore. Love doesn't erase trauma; it just gives it context. The goal isn't to fix them. It's to meet them where they are and stay there.

At some point you'll hit the wall. The dog's progress stalls. You're tired, guilty, frustrated. You'll think about returning them. Then you'll hate yourself for it. That's normal. Every rescuer feels it. It's called compassion fatigue, and it's real. Take a breath. Get help. Trainers and behaviorists aren't proof of failure; they're proof you give a damn.

Some rescues need more than love and routine. Fear aggression, severe separation anxiety, food guarding—these don't vanish with "good vibes." Hire a pro. A solid trainer or vet behaviorist can save your sanity and your furniture. Asking for help isn't weakness; it's strategy.

Even when things smooth out, regression happens. Move houses, have a baby, change work hours—bam, old anxieties resurface. That's not betrayal; it's memory. You remind them, gently, that this home still stands. That consistency outlasts chaos. A year in, you'll realize you stopped noticing the scars. They've blended into normal life. That's when you've truly succeeded.

Add kids or other pets, and the stakes double. Do it slow. Controlled intros. No free-for-alls. Watch body language. Rescue Labs are tolerant, not bulletproof. "He's fine" is not a plan. Teach children to speak softly, respect space, and quit the grab-and-hug routine. Jealousy is real. Feed separately. Rotate toys. Give equal attention. Labs are emotional sponges; they'll mirror the household vibe. If you're tense, so are they.

The easiest way to ruin progress is pity parenting—dropping boundaries because you "feel bad." That's how affection turns into chaos. Dogs don't heal through indulgence. They heal through structure, predictability, and fairness. You're not making up for their past; you're building a future.

And then, out of nowhere, it happens. The dog looks up mid-walk, tail wagging, eyes soft, shoulders loose. They stop scanning for exits. That's the moment they decide you're real. It won't look like a movie. It'll look ordinary—but it'll wreck you anyway. I've seen it hundreds of times. The first head tilt. The first time they fall asleep against you instead of beside the door. The first unguarded sigh. That's when the job title changes from rescuer to partner.

I once worked with a Lab named Diesel who'd spent two years tied to a tree. The chain had worn a groove into his neck, and his spirit was long gone. For months he wouldn't make eye contact. Then one night during a storm, lightning cracked and he dove into my lap shaking. That was the first time he touched me on purpose. He didn't move for an hour. I didn't either. Six months later, that same dog was retrieving bumpers in a lake, tail spinning like a propeller. Redemption doesn't come with trumpets; it comes with a sigh of relief.

Even "fixed" rescues need upkeep. Keep training, keep boundaries, keep vet checks. Age doesn't erase fear—it just buries it. Stay consistent. They'll trust you longer than they trusted anyone else, but only if you keep earning it.

Rescue exposes your flaws faster than therapy. If you're impatient, they'll show it. If you're anxious, they'll reflect it. You learn emotional regulation because your dog forces you to. They don't need a perfect human; they need a stable one. Funny how those two end up being the same thing after a while.

The first time they crawl into your lap uninvited, or wag when you come home without hesitation, you'll understand why people keep doing this even after it breaks their hearts. It's not gratitude they give you—it's trust. And it's worth everything.

Rescue doesn't make you better than other owners. It just makes you real. You stop bragging, start noticing small wins. You measure success in calm naps and clean bowls instead of Instagram likes. You lie on the floor beside them because they finally feel safe enough to sleep deep. That's not pity. That's peace.

So yes, second-chance Labs will test you. They'll push, chew, panic, and sometimes scare you. But when they finally look at you without fear—when they lean in and stay—that's the payoff no breeder can sell and no training class can promise. They don't care who you were before. They only care who you are now. If you show up every day, steady and honest, they'll give you everything they have left.

That's what a second chance really is. Not rescue. Not redemption. Partnership—earned the hard way, loved without condition, and remembered long after the fur fades.

Chapter 19
Leash in Hand: You Made the Dog.
Now Be Worth It.

If you've made it this far, congratulations. Seriously…congratulations. Because this book wasn't written to pet your ego or sell you a dream of golden fur glowing in a sunset. It was written to tell you the truth. Every last messy, muddy, hair-covered, tail-whipping bit of it.

You've read about the price, the pressure, the noise. You've seen the wreckage: shredded shoes, demolished couches, the puddles that defy physics. You've trudged through the land-shark phase and the sleepless nights. And you're still here—still holding the leash. That means something.

It means you didn't give up when it got hard. It means you didn't dump your dog at the first sign of chaos. It means you learned to find beauty in the disaster. You stuck it out through the shedding and the slobber and the endless need for motion. That makes you part of a rare species yourself: a human who actually finished what they started.

The real beginning of owning a Lab isn't the day you brought the puppy home, or the day they finally stopped eating drywall. It's the moment you realized this wasn't about "training a dog." It's about becoming someone worth following.

Labs will follow you anywhere—but only because they believe you're worth it. They don't obey out of fear or worship. They obey because you've earned their faith. You became the one steady voice in a world that moves too fast.

You gave them structure, and they gave you their whole damn heart.

That's the deal.

A Labrador doesn't challenge you like a Rottweiler does, but they test you in quieter ways. They test your patience, your consistency, your ability to say no to the eyes that could bankrupt your soul. They'll charm you into laziness, guilt you into overfeeding, and teach you the cost of skipping boundaries. They'll make you confront the difference between loving a dog and leading one.

You can't fake leadership with a Lab. You can't baby them into good behavior or bribe them into sanity. They're too smart and too sensitive for shortcuts. They read tone faster than commands, moods faster than words. If you're calm, they're calm. If you're frantic, they'll turn it into a circus. They are emotional mirrors with paws, and they reflect whatever chaos you bring to the room.

There are no hacks here. No magic collars. No miracle toys. Just time, repetition, and honesty. Labs demand fairness. They need exercise like oxygen and structure like faith. Miss either one, and you'll meet the gremlin inside the golden smile.

Because that's what real leadership is—showing up every day, even when it's inconvenient. Especially then. You don't get a break just because you're tired. You built the expectation. You keep the standard. That's how trust works, and that's how this breed thrives.

Labs don't need drill sergeants or best friends. They need partners. They need someone who understands that love without rules is chaos, and discipline without compassion is cruelty. They don't need perfection; they need presence.

You don't *own* a Lab—you share your life with one. They'll drag you into lakes, steal your sandwich, and force you to notice the world again. They'll remind you that joy is messy and patience is earned. They'll break your things and fix your soul, often on the same day.

And if you screw it up, they won't bite or bolt—they'll wilt. They'll shut down quietly, the way only sensitive dogs can. That's when you realize the power you hold isn't physical—it's emotional. You can either build them up or break them down. There's no middle ground.

That's the responsibility every Lab owner carries. The world sees the friendly smile, the wagging tail, the "safe family dog." What they don't see is how fragile that reputation is. Every neglected, untrained, or overweight Lab adds another crack in it. Every time one ends up in a shelter because someone "didn't realize how much work they are," the whole breed pays the price.

It's not fair. But it's real.

So we train. We walk. We swim. We monitor food, trim nails, clean ears, and throw the damn ball a hundred times a day because that's what we signed up for. We give them outlets so their instincts don't become problems. We proof recall, because freedom without control is a death sentence. We teach calm at the door, leave-it in the kitchen, and off-switch in the yard. We do the boring work that no one applauds because we know what happens when people don't.

That's the weight of loving a Lab. They'll give you everything, but you have to earn the right to hold it. They'll follow you into freezing water, guard your kids, and sleep beside you like breathing shadows. All they ask is that you lead them well.

That's the thing most people never understand until they've lived it. This isn't just about obedience or manners. It's about who you become in the process. You learn to slow down. To be patient. To laugh when everything's covered in fur and water. To love something enough to stay consistent even when you're exhausted.

That version of you—the one who shows up, who keeps trying, who balances structure with humor—that's the person your dog believes in. That's the human worth following.

And one day, after years of training, mistakes, forgiveness, and miles of leash, you'll call their name across a field, and they'll turn and come flying back like it's the best idea they've ever had. That's when it hits you—you built that. Every rep, every rule, every ounce of trust.

You did this.
You made this dog.

And in doing it, you made yourself better.

Labs don't just leave hair on your clothes or dents in your drywall. They leave handprints on your habits. They rewrite your patience, sharpen your empathy, and teach you what loyalty actually looks like. They make you stronger and softer at the same time.

So here you are, leash in hand, standing at the edge of everything you've learned. Maybe your dog's at your feet right now, waiting for what's next. Maybe they're still a puppy chewing on your last nerve. Maybe they're gone, and the leash just feels heavier now.

Wherever you are, this is the moment. Not to have it all figured out, but to commit. For real. To say, "I'll keep showing up. I'll keep learning. I'll do right by this dog."

That's all they've ever asked. Not perfection. Just presence.

So take the leash.
Step forward.
You've got a Labrador now.
And they're watching.

WELCOME TO THE BEST AND WORST DECISION OF YOUR LIFE

So. You made it through.

You read the warnings. You stared down the price tags, the training drills, the shedding apocalypse, the ear-infection horror stories, the "he ate WHAT?" moments. You trudged through puppy madness, rescue heartbreak, and the thousand ways Labs can turn good intentions into disaster.

And you're still here. Still thinking this breed might be for you. Still looking at the shredded hoodie and the drool-covered walls like, yeah, worth it. Still saying, "Okay... what's next?"

Here's what's next: you either rise to the occasion, or your Labrador becomes another shelter statistic. There's no middle ground. No "we'll figure it out." No "he'll calm down eventually." He won't. He'll grow into the chaos you allow. Into the habits you reinforce. Into the leadership you give—or don't.

If you fail him, he won't turn dangerous; he'll turn broken. Depressed. Destructive. Because Labs don't go rogue—they go bored, under-exercised, under-stimulated, and under-led. And that's on you.

But if you get it right? If you grind through the 5 a.m. walks and the 10 p.m. clean-ups, the crate crying, the leash tangles, the chewed remotes, the guilt, the embarrassment, and the exhaustion. If you train through the madness instead of excusing it. If you show up every day, rain or shine, patience barely holding together, but still there. You'll get the real thing.

Not the Instagram prop or the "family-friendly" ad campaign dog. You'll get a partner. The one who watches your every move because you matter that much. The one who retrieves a toy, a duck, or your sanity with the same intensity. The one who reads you better than most humans do.

You'll get the dog who makes people laugh in the park, who charms the vet tech, who disarms even the crankiest neighbor. The dog who charges into a lake like it owes him money and comes back with a stick, a shoe, and half a waterfowl population. The dog who sleeps across your feet like an anchor because in his mind, you're the whole damn world.

And here's the truth no one tells you: you didn't just train that. You earned it.

Every chew mark, every muddy pawprint, every "oh god, not again" moment forged something real. You became the kind of human a Labrador deserves—consistent, patient, fair. You became the leader who shows up. The one who means it.

Because Labs don't need perfection; they need presence. They don't need fancy tools; they need your time. They don't want control; they want connection. They'll give you everything they have if you just prove you can handle it.

That's what makes them both the best and worst decision of your life.

They'll drive you insane. They'll test your limits. They'll make you question your choices, your sanity, your furniture budget. But then—when they finally settle their head on your knee after a long day, eyes heavy, tail thumping once— you'll realize it was all worth it. Every ruined shoe, every sleepless night, every swear word.

Because that moment? That's peace in fur. That's loyalty in motion. That's love, honest and loud and a little damp.

If this book scared you off, good. It should have. Labs aren't for everyone. They're too much for most. Too smart. Too needy. Too full of themselves. But for the people who can match that energy—who don't flinch at the work, who get that chaos and devotion are two sides of the same coin— they're everything.

So if you're still standing here, leash in hand, hair on your clothes, wallet lighter, heart heavier, and saying, "Let's go"?

Then welcome. You've made the best worst decision of your life. And the Labrador will make sure you never regret it.

APPENDIX A
NEW OWNER SURVIVAL CHECKLIST
IF YOU'RE MISSING THESE, RETURN THE DOG

Congratulations, you did it. You brought home a Labrador, the furry embodiment of chaos, obsession, and digestive mystery. The next thirty days will test your patience, your reflexes, your plumbing, and your sense of humor. You are now responsible for an animal that will eat drywall, drink puddles, and shed in ways that defy known physics.

If you're not prepared, the dog will win. This checklist is here to make sure you don't end up crying in your hallway at 3 a.m. surrounded by shredded paper towels and regret.

Gear You Actually Need (a.k.a. The Stuff That Keeps You Sane)

- **Crate** - Your dog's house. Your only hope. It's not a jail; it's a reset button for chaos. Use it early, use it often, and use it without guilt. The people who say "crates are cruel" also have chewed baseboards and dogs that pee on Amazon deliveries.

- **Two Leashes** - Yes, two. One for normal life and one for the moment your Lab discovers flight. You'll think one's enough until you drop it and watch your dog gallop toward the horizon like a Pixar sequel gone wrong.

- **Harness** - Because Labs pull like they're training for the Iditarod. A proper front-clip harness saves your shoulders and your dignity. Bonus: it prevents that full-body lunge toward every bird, bug, and sandwich within range.

- **Chew Rotation Arsenal** - You don't own chew toys; you manage a rotation schedule. Kongs, ropes, frozen washcloths, bones, puzzle feeders—swap them daily or your Lab will improvise with something electrical.

- **Poop Bags** - Buy in bulk. Then buy more. There's nothing like watching your dog squat majestically in public and realizing your last bag was yesterday.

- **Cleaning Supplies** - Enzymatic cleaner for the carpet. Paper towels for your tears. A mop that can handle existential crises. Bonus points for air freshener strong enough to erase the scent of wet Labrador.

- **High-Value Treats** - Your bribe currency. You'll need them for crate training, recall, and surviving puppy class without public humiliation. Choose something that doesn't turn to dust in your pocket and doesn't smell like roadkill.

- **Food & Water Bowls (Heavy Ones)** - Because Labs treat eating like a sport. Lightweight bowls end up halfway across the kitchen. Get stainless steel. Dishwasher safe. Indestructible.

- **Baby Gates** - Labs have zero impulse control. A good gate saves your sanity, your shoes, and whatever's cooking on the counter. Bonus: keeps toddlers alive too.

- **ID Tag & Microchip** - Your dog will bolt. Maybe not today, maybe not tomorrow—but the first time you drop a fry, he's gone. Make sure whoever finds him can call you before animal control does.

- **Patience (Non-Refundable)** - You can't buy it, but you'll spend it daily. The good news? It regenerates faster than your throw pillows.

Appendix B
Training & Socialization Timeline—
Because Time Doesn't Wait for Chaos

Think of this as your "Oh God, am I behind?" chart. Labs grow fast, mature slow, and learn constantly. Miss a phase, and you're playing catch-up with eighty pounds of enthusiasm.

Age	Milestone	Translation
8–10 Weeks	Crate training begins. Introduce leash, short car rides, gentle handling.	You're teaching them life isn't chaos 24/7. Good luck.
10–14 Weeks	Socialization sprint. People, dogs, sounds, surfaces, vets.	You're late if they're still afraid of the vacuum.
3–6 Months	Basic obedience. Sit, stay, come, down, leave it.	Congratulations, you're raising a toddler with teeth.
6–9 Months	Adolescence meltdown. Regression, boundary testing, selective hearing.	Welcome to the hormonal apocalypse. Don't quit now.
9–12 Months	Impulse control training, leash manners, structured play.	"Calm" isn't genetic; it's a full-time job.
1–2 Years	Consistency phase. Advanced training, recall proofing, endurance work.	The chaos starts making sense. You're almost human again.
2+ Years	Maintenance mode. Health routines, mental work, social refreshers.	The Labrador you dreamed of finally shows up. Don't ruin it.

Missed a Step? Here's How to Recover Without Losing Your Mind:

If your Lab's already learned a few bad habits—chewing, jumping, counter-surfing, or selective deafness—don't panic. Regression is normal. Labs push buttons just to see if they still work. Go back to structure, reintroduce the crate, up the exercise, and tighten your routine. You can fix almost anything with time, consistency, and snacks that smell like regret.

Appendix C
Health Red Flags Quick Guide — Vet Now vs. Google Later

If you live with a Labrador, you'll eventually have a panic moment — something gross, weird, or alarming that makes you type "is my dog dying" into Google at 2 a.m. while your dog sleeps peacefully beside you, farting.

This guide exists to stop that spiral. Because Labs are dramatic little tanks: they can look fine while quietly imploding, or look like death when it's just a grass burp. Here's your quick triage: what needs a vet *now*, what to *monitor*, and what to *stop overreacting* about.

Emergency Color Code:

⬤ **RED = VET NOW** (drop everything, grab the leash, and drive)

⬤ **YELLOW = Monitor Closely** (take notes, watch patterns, call if it worsens)

⬤ **GREEN = Stop Googling** (you're fine, your dog's fine, your anxiety isn't)

Symptom	What's Actually Going On	Action Code	Translation
Non-stop vomiting (more than twice, or anything with blood)	Possible blockage, poisoning, or stomach twist.	⬤	**Get in the damn car.** Labs eat socks for sport.
Distended belly, pacing, drooling, can't lie down	Classic signs of bloat (GDV) — especially deadly for big Labs.	⬤	**Every minute counts.** Don't "wait and see."

Symptom	What's Actually Going On	Action Code	Translation
Limping or refusal to bear weight	Injury, torn ligament, hip or elbow flare-up.	● → ● if it lasts more than 24 hrs or dog cries.	You're not "babying" them. You're preventing surgery bills.
Thick, brown, or yeasty ear gunk	Infection, moisture, allergies — a Lab's favorite hobby.	●	Clean what you can, see vet for meds. Stop using baby wipes.
Hot spots, red skin, constant itching	Allergies, fleas, or boredom.	●	Bathe, use medicated shampoo, call vet if it spreads or oozes.
Sudden loss of appetite or refusal to eat for 24 hours	Dental pain, upset stomach, or something worse.	● if paired with vomiting or lethargy.	"Labs never skip a meal", if they do, panic is valid.
Lab looks tired, wobbly, or weak	Could be overheating, dehydration, or internal issue.	●	Heat stroke kills fast. Cool with water, call the vet en route.
Coughing, gagging, or hacking after water	Could be kennel cough or water aspiration.	●	Note timing and sound. Call vet if persistent. Don't WebMD it.
Excessive drinking or peeing	Early kidney issue, diabetes, or boredom habit.	● → ● if sudden or paired with weight loss.	Not "just thirsty." Something's off.
Scooting or butt licking	Anal glands or worms.	●	Gross, but normal. Get them expressed, not exorcised.

Symptom	What's Actually Going On	Action Code	Translation
Occasional soft stool	Diet change, stress, or that mystery sock.	●	Monitor. If it turns to soup or blood, upgrade to ●.
Eye discharge or redness	Mild irritation or early infection.	●	Wipe gently, **no Visine**, vet if worsening.
Constant head shaking	Ear infection or foreign object.	●	Common, fixable. Don't let it fester into surgery.
Constant head shaking	Heat stroke, bloat, seizure, cardiac event.	●	Don't Google. Don't post. DRIVE.

Visual Flow (a.k.a. The Panic Decision Tree)

Something's wrong →
→ *Is your dog breathing and responsive?*
  No → **Call Emergency Vet NOW.**
  Yes → Move down the check list

→ *Are they vomiting, bloated, bleeding, or refusing to move?*
  Yes → **Vet NOW (Red Zone).**
  No → Move down the check list

→ *Are they acting "off?" Limping, scratching, shaking, or ignoring food?*
    Yes → **Monitor Closely (Yellow Zone).**
    No → Move down the check list

→ *Are they otherwise normal but doing something gross?*
    Yes → **Stop Googling (Green Zone).**
    Clean it up. Move on.

Zero Woofs Reminder:

Labs don't fake symptoms. If something feels wrong, it probably is. But also—don't panic every time they cough.

These dogs eat rocks for breakfast and survive. Your job is to know when they *shouldn't have.*

Keep your vet's number posted on the fridge. Save the after-hours emergency clinic in your phone. And for the love of dogs: if your Lab looks like they're in trouble, stop scrolling and start driving.

Appendix D
Travel & Boarding Checklist — How to Keep Your Dog (and Your Sitter) Alive

So you're leaving your Labrador in someone else's care. Brave. Whether it's a weekend getaway, a road trip, or just a desperate attempt to remember what silence sounds like, one thing's guaranteed: your dog will act like they've never met a rule in their life.

This list exists so your sitter, friend, or unsuspecting relative doesn't panic, cry, or fake their own death mid-weekend.

Packing List for the Chaos on Four Legs

☐ **Food (Enough + Extra)** - Bring at least two days more than you think you'll need. You'll thank yourself when flights get delayed or your Lab suddenly develops Olympic-level hunger. Label it clearly. "One scoop, twice a day" does *not* mean "let him free-feed because he looks sad."

☐ **Feeding Schedule** - Write it down like you're leaving instructions for a nuclear reactor. Include portions, treat rules, and any "don't you dare give him table scraps" warnings. Labs are professional con artists — protect your sitter from manipulation.

☐ **Leash, Collar, and Backup Leash** - Because the one you brought will break when your Lab sees a squirrel the size of a keychain. Always pack a spare. Always.

☐ **Harness** - Front-clip, well-fitted, labeled if possible. Your sitter shouldn't have to Google "how to put on a dog harness" while your Lab attempts to eat the instructions.

☐ **Crate or Bed** - Familiar space = fewer meltdowns. Bring their own bedding, even if it smells like a swamp. That smell is comfort. Gross comfort, but comfort.

☐ **Favorite Toys** - Two to three maximum. Too many, and your sitter will spend the weekend stepping on soggy plushies. Include one chew toy, one comfort toy, and one "if all else fails" distraction.

☐ **Medications & Supplements** - Label everything clearly. Include dosage, timing, and what happens if they miss a dose. Tape a copy of your vet's info to the bottle. If the meds are in a peanut-butter-delivery system, note that too.

☐ **Emergency Contacts** - Vet, emergency vet, backup contact (because you'll be unreachable in a mountain cabin "finding yourself"), and your own number — even if you *swear* you'll check your phone.

☐ **Vaccination & ID Info** - Printed. Not digital. The Wi-Fi will fail exactly when your sitter needs to prove your dog isn't Patient Zero.

☐ **Cleaning Supplies** - Because your Lab will not have diarrhea until the moment you leave. Enzymatic spray, paper towels, and a box of "emotional support" garbage bags.

☐ **Anxiety Notes** - Does your dog lose their mind during thunderstorms, car rides, or when someone sneezes wrong? Write that down. Also note your go-to fixes: a frozen Kong, a walk, or the sacred phrase "wanna cookie?"

☐ **Command List** - Every Lab owner uses different cues. If you say "drop it" and your sitter says "leave it," guess who's winning that argument? Not the human.

☐ **Travel Water Bottle / Collapsible Bowl** - Hydration saves lives (and car upholstery).

☐ **Poop Bags** - Don't assume your sitter has any. You're not the only one living this glamorous life.

Quick Note for Road Trips

- Stop every 2–3 hours.
- Bring towels for the inevitable "random puddle dive."
- Keep the AC strong — Labs cook fast.
- Never, ever leave them in the car. Not even "just for a minute." You'll come back to a heatstroke and a felony.

For Boarding Facilities

- Drop off early in the day. That gives your Lab time to adjust before bedtime.

- Leave quietly. No emotional Oscar performance at the gate. Your guilt makes it worse.

- Bring their regular food and some of your dirty laundry. It's weirdly comforting.

- Tell the staff about quirks: "He guards tennis balls," "She hates mops," "He'll fake limp for treats."

"How to Bribe Your Dog Sitter So They'll Ever Do This Again"

1. Leave snacks. Human snacks. Good ones. Chocolate, wine, coffee, whatever their poison.

2. Pre-pay. You're not hiring a volunteer; you're hiring a survivalist.

3. Leave a handwritten thank-you note that says, "If he vomits up another sock, just call the vet — not me."

4. Venmo them hazard pay if your Lab decides to test their limit on obedience, digestion, or gravity.

Zero Woofs Reminder:

Your Labrador will always act 20% worse the second you walk out the door. It's science. Preparation is the only thing standing between your sitter and a nervous breakdown.

Double-check this list, hand over the leash, and remember: anyone willing to watch your Lab twice deserves a medal — or at least a bottle of something strong.

Appendix E
Emergency Contacts Page —
Because Chaos Has a Schedule

When disaster hits, and it will, it won't be during business hours. It'll be at 11:47 p.m., in the rain, while your Lab is foaming at the mouth from eating a mystery "snack" you told them to leave.

This page exists because your brain will short-circuit under pressure. Fill it out, print it, tape it inside a cabinet, and give a copy to anyone who might end up babysitting your chaos gremlin. Don't rely on your phone; it'll die at 3 percent battery right when you need it most.

Primary Veterinarian

Clinic Name: _____

Vet's Name: _____

Phone: _____

Address: _____

After-Hours Instructions: _____
Notes:
Hours, quirks, and the receptionist who secretly runs the place.
Example: "Ask for Kim; she knows the hip history."

Emergency Vet Hospital

Clinic Name: _____

Phone (24 hr): _____

Address: _____

Directions from Home: _____

Notes:

List closest 24/7 hospital *and* an alternate. Because your GPS will crash the second you panic.

Animal Poison Control Hotlines

ASPCA Poison Control: (888) 426-4435 (*fee may apply*)

Pet Poison Helpline: (855) 764-7661

What to Know Before Calling:

Have the **product label** or **substance name** ready.

Know your dog's **weight** and **approximate ingestion time**.

Don't make them throw up unless a professional says so. Your Lab has already suffered enough indignity for one day.

Trainer / Behavior Consultant

Name: _____

Phone: _____

Email: _____

Notes:

For when the "just a phase" becomes an exorcism.

Backup Dog Sitter / Trusted Friend

Name: _____

Phone: _____

Address: _____

Spare Key Location: _____

Notes:

Make sure this person actually likes your dog. Not everyone thinks 90 pounds of drool and desperation is "cute."

Groomer / Boarding Facility Contact (Optional)

Name: _____

Phone: _____

Address: _____

Notes:

Include this if your Lab has a regular spot. The staff will remember exactly which towel they shredded last visit.

Miscellaneous Information

Microchip Number: _____

Registration Company: _____

Insurance Provider: _____

Policy Number: _____

Allergies / Known Health Issues: _____

Medications & Dosages: _____

Behavior Triggers / Warnings: _____

(Examples: Hates thunder, barks at men in hats, believes mail carriers are Satan.)

Zero Woofs Reminder:

Panic is a luxury you don't get when you own a Labrador.
Write this stuff down *before* you need it.
Tape it to your fridge.
Screenshot it on your phone.
Hand a copy to anyone who ever touches your dog.
Because chaos has a schedule.
And your Lab will always book the 3 a.m. slot.

Appendix F

Recommended Resources: real trainers, rescue orgs, and products that don't suck.

You've read the book, survived the chaos, and maybe, just maybe, you're ready to take this Lab thing seriously.
This is the part where most "breed guides" start hawking miracle gadgets and treat brands that taste like despair.
Not here.
Everything on this list is either field-tested, trainer-approved, or survived direct contact with an actual Labrador.

Trainers Who Know Their Shit
(aka, people who don't clap for mediocrity)
* **K9 Lifeline (Utah, USA)**
  Balanced, real-world training. Not a treat-tossing circus. Great for reactivity, impulse control, and reality checks.
* **The Canine Paradigm (Australia)**
  Podcast + community of working-dog trainers who speak fluent chaos. If you want to understand drive, this is your church.
* **Leerburg Online University**
  Old-school, no-frills, brutally practical. Their foundation videos on obedience and engagement are gold for working breeds.
* **Larry Krohn — "The Good Dog Way"**
  Straight talk, solid results. Especially good for Labs with selective hearing and Olympic-level enthusiasm.
* **Jeff Gellman / Solid K9 Training**
  Blunt, effective, zero sugarcoating. Watch if you want honesty over hugs.

Rescue & Rehome Organizations That Deserve Your Money

- **Labrador Retriever Rescue, Inc. (LRR)**
  Covers multiple U.S. regions. Real screening, real follow-up, and zero tolerance for impulse adopters.
- **The Labrador Lifeline Trust (UK)**
  Rehomes Labs with compassion and competence. They don't post sob stories—they post results.
- **Retriever Rescue of Colorado**
  Takes in the overbred, the misunderstood, and the "oops" litters. Transparent, ethical, and full of heart.
- **Your Local Shelter (seriously)**
  There's probably a Lab sitting there right now. He's perfect, he's loud, and he deserves better than your HOA.

Breeders Who Actually Care

(Yes, they exist. No, you won't find them on Craigslist.)
Look for these red flags to avoid instead of specific names:
Won't show health certificates for hips, elbows, and eyes.
Breeds for color ("rare silver Labs!") instead of function.
"Family raised" but never mentions working aptitude or titles.
No contract. No questions. Just cash. Run.
Ask for breeders affiliated with:
The Labrador Retriever Club (AKC Parent Club) — Health-tested, breed-purpose focused.
UK Kennel Club Assured Breeder Scheme — Not perfect, but at least it's got standards.
A good breeder interrogates you like the CIA. If they don't, that's your red flag.

Tools & Products That Don't Fall Apart (or Lie)

Training Gear
- *Herm Sprenger prong collar*: if you know how to use it, it's communication, not cruelty.
- *Mendota slip lead*: field-tested, nearly indestructible.
- *Fi GPS Collar*: for when "he never runs off" becomes famous last words.
- *Ruffwear Front Range Harness*: durable, adjustable, Labrador-proof.

Feeding & Health
- *Purina Pro Plan*: the only big-brand kibble that consistently survives ingredient scrutiny.

- *TruDog dental spray*: it works. Yes, really.
- *Omega-3 supplements (Grizzly or Zesty Paws)*: your Lab's joints will thank you.

Grooming & Cleanup
- *Furminator or SleekEZ*: your vacuum's only chance.
- *Zymox Ear Solution*: for the eternal swamp ears.
- *Nature's Miracle Advanced*: because Labs poop creatively.
- *Bissell CrossWave Pet Pro*: a vacuum built for emotional trauma.

Enrichment & Sanity-Savers
- *KONG Extreme*: the only toy that survives adolescence.
- *West Paw Toppl*: enrichment toy that doubles as a peace offering.
- *Outward Hound Puzzle Feeders*: slows the "inhale now, regret later" feeding style.
- *Chuckit! Launcher*: because your shoulder deserves better.

Books That Tell the Truth (and Don't Smell Like BS)
- *The Culture Clash* by Jean Donaldson — honest, behavioral reality check.
- *Don't Shoot the Dog!* by Karen Pryor — foundational positive training.
- *No Bad Dogs* by Barbara Woodhouse — old-school but legendary.
- *The Labrador Retriever Handbook* by Pippa Mattinson — actually useful, not Pinterest fluff.

Online Communities Worth Your Time
- **"Zero Woofs Given" Facebook Group (coming soon)**: Real dog people, real stories, zero tolerance for "fur baby" nonsense.
- **r/dogs (Reddit)**: Hit or miss, but solid for second opinions and venting.
- **r/labrador**: Full of photo spam, but occasionally someone says something intelligent.
- **Working Dog Forums**: If you want to understand what your Lab *could* be instead of what pet culture turned it into.

QR Shortcut Page (Design Note)
- Include a clean layout with scannable QR codes linking to:
- Trainer websites

- Product affiliate-free pages
- Rescue orgs
- Recommended book list on ZeroWoofsGiven.com

Zero Woofs Reminder:
You don't need the fanciest gear, the trendiest trainer, or the priciest food.
You just need the stuff that works.
If it survives your Lab for six months, it's worth recommending.
If it doesn't, bury it with honors in the backyard and move on.

ABOUT THE AUTHOR

Zero Woofs Given was born out of one sarcastic human's lifelong gripe with the sugarcoated nonsense in dog books.

Founded by Shannon, a snarky, lifelong dog devotee and proud Rottweiler mom to Rowan and Rip, has spent 20+ years knee-deep in fur, mud, training sessions, and vet clinic exam rooms, surviving the kind of chaos only a determined canine can create. From rescue work to breed-specific research, she's seen the best, worst, and most unhinged sides of dog ownership and lived to write about it.

Shannon's mission is blunt: when people pick the wrong dog, the dog pays the price. They end up in shelters for being exactly what they were bred to be...while humans fail them. Her guides exist to stop that cycle.

When not writing, she's wrangling her own four-legged disasters, dodging drool, and questioning life choices while still believing there's no better companion than a dog with a heartbeat and zero manners.

Zero Woofs Given Press exists for one reason: to torch the sugarcoated garbage. These books won't tell you every dog "loves kids" or "thrives in apartments." They'll tell you the messy, hilarious, heartbreaking truth, so you know what you're getting into before your shoes, furniture, and sanity are destroyed.

Thank You

You picked up a book about Labrador Retrievers, which means you either have one, want one, or you've already lost a shoe to one and need answers. Either way...respect.

Writing these guides isn't about making you feel warm and fuzzy; it's about making sure you understand that living with a Lab is equal parts comedy show and demolition derby.

If this book stopped you from thinking a Lab would magically raise your kids, gave you a fighting chance at channeling their endless energy into something besides chewing drywall, or at least made you laugh while yours body-slammed you for the tennis ball, then it did its job.

Here's the truth: Labs aren't "perfect family dogs" by default. They're driven, energetic, mouthy, stubborn, and smarter than most of the humans who own them. The problem isn't the breed—it's people treating a working dog like a plush toy. My mission is to stop that cycle, save a few couches, and keep more Labs out of shelters.

Want more of this kind of brutal honesty? Sign up for *The Feral Dispatch* newsletter at ZeroWoofsGiven.com.

It's the only place you'll get fresh doses of unfiltered dog truth, weekly chaos, and the occasional reminder that your dog is normal...it's the humans who are messed up.

While you're there, check out the rest of the Zero Woofs Given Dog Breed Library. Every guide is just as blunt, just as sarcastic, and just as likely to save your furniture and your sanity.

And if you've decided maybe a Lab isn't for you (or you'd like to see what other chaos is brewing), hit our Dog Breed Profile page on the website. It's packed with early-access snippets of guides still in the works, so you can get the unfiltered truth before the full book drops.

So, thanks for showing up for the raw version, not the sugarcoated bullshit. You're the reason this series exists and maybe the reason your Lab doesn't eat the neighbors.

BIBLIOGRAPHY

American Kennel Club. (n.d.). Labrador Retriever Dog Breed Information. https://www.akc.org/dog-breeds/labrador-retriever/

Coile, C. (2024, October 28). Labrador Retriever | Characteristics, History, & Facts. Encyclopedia Britannica. https://www.britannica.com/animal/Labrador-retriever

Diener, M., DVM. (2024, May 29). Labrador Retriever. https://www.petmd.com/dog/breeds/labrador-retriever

DogTime. (2024, October 25). Labrador Retriever. DogTime. https://dogtime.com/dog-breeds/labrador-retriever

Keeping Your Labrador Retriever Healthy: A Guide to Common Health Concerns – ImpriMed. (n.d.). https://www.imprimedicine.com/blog/labrador-retriever

The Labrador Retriever Club, Inc. (2024, May 10). Home - The Labrador Retriever Club, Inc. https://thelabradorclub.com/

Training a young labrador retriever-part 1 | Training | Gundog Journal. (2020, April 29). Gundog Journal. https://gundog-journal.com/training-and-advice/training-a-young-labrador-retriever-%E2%80%93-part-1

Venzel, S., & Venzel, S. (2022, January 13). What Causes Labradors Colors, Including The Famous "Silver Lab." Wide Open Spaces. https://www.wideopenspaces.com/labrador-colors/

Wikipedia contributors. (2024, October 10). Labrador Retriever. Wikipedia. https://en.wikipedia.org/wiki/Labrador_Retriever